GRITS
TO
GLORY

GRITS
TO
GLORY

How Southern Cookin' Got So Good

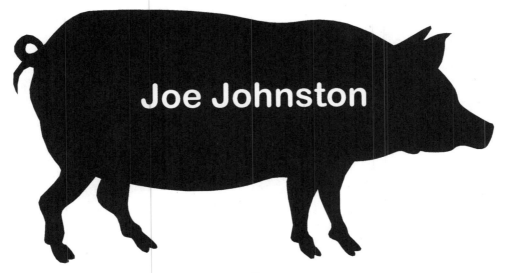

Joe Johnston

PELICAN PUBLISHING COMPANY
GRETNA 2018

The word "Pelican" and the depiction of a pelican are trademarks of Pelican Publishing Company, Inc., and are registered in the U.S. Patent and Trademark Office.

Library of Congress Cataloging-in-Publication Data

Names: Johnston, Joe, 1948- author.
Title: Grits to glory : how Southern cookin got so good / by Joe Johnston.
Description: Gretna, Louisiana : Pelican Publishing Company, Inc., [2018] |
   Includes bibliographical references and index.
Identifiers: LCCN 2017048665| ISBN 9781455624034 (pbk. : alk. paper) | ISBN
   9781455624041 (ebook)
Subjects: LCSH: Cooking, American--Southern style. | Cooking--Southern
   States. | LCGFT: Cookbooks.
Classification: LCC TX715.2.S68 J644 2018 | DDC 641.5975--dc23 LC record available at https://
lccn.loc.gov/2017048665

Printed in the United States of America

Published by Pelican Publishing Company, Inc.
1000 Burmaster Street, Gretna, Louisiana 70053
www.pelicanpub.com

Dedicated to my sons, Luke and Will, men of taste

Contents

Many men, like this army cook, learned during the Civil War how to acquire, preserve, and cook food. That knowledge was precious when they returned home. (Courtesy of Library of Congress)

Acknowledgements

This book wouldn't have been possible without the countless contributions of my wonderful wife, Rebecca Asling Johnston, cook, hostess, and a daughter of Oklahoma, Arkansas, Tennessee, and North Carolina.

Thanks for heirloom recipes, photos, and stories to: Tanya Touchstone for the Branson and Simpson families; Michael Barham for Mama Ruth's kitchen; Jan Davies Weinheimer for Pearl Cole Davies; Patty Tingley Sisco for Lizzie Morris Tingley; Laurel Kelsey Wells for Ella Armstrong; Dawne Davis for Blanche Davis; Rhonda Lee for Choctaw heritage, the Fosters, and the Hunsakers; Marsha Jenkins for the Casey family; and Jay Weinheimer for the best ribs in town and his carp recipe. My deep gratitude to Pearl Moon Stanfield and Elaine Stanfield for stories and recipes that span many miles and generations. Special thanks to Perma Harris, reader.

I learned to love this history by watching and listening to my mother, Jaunita Johnston. And I'm grateful to my Marsden, Hargrove, Tully, Ahern, London, and Glanzner cousins for keeping this history alive.

A special thank you to the editor-in-chief, Nina Kooij, and my editor, Eugenie Brignac, and Pelican Publishing Company for believing this story needs to be told.

Photos not otherwise credited are from my collection.

The Dennis family of Nashville gathers around the table after church and a big meal to share card games, love, and laughter. (Courtesy of Debbie Smartt)

Introduction

One evening when I was a kid, I walked down the street with my parents for dinner at Harden's Hamburgers. While we were eating our burgers and fries, I noticed a man I'd never seen before back in the kitchen. He was a stocky, white-haired, older fellow with a white mustache and goatee, and under his apron he wore a white shirt with a black string tie like the ones I'd seen in western movies. "Who's that?" I asked the waitress, Addy.

"That's a man from Kentucky, Colonel Sanders, he calls himself. He's trying to sell us his fried chicken recipe," Addy sneered. We all laughed. Trying to sell a fried chicken recipe to a burger place!

The Colonel was standing over the stove, and I could see a tray of golden chicken on the counter beside him. Pretty soon Johnny Harden walked around with the tray, introduced us to the Colonel, and offered everyone in the place a piece. Then they came back around to ask what we all thought. They honestly wanted to know, so we told them it was delicious. A week or so later, Johnny started serving the Colonel's chicken, as did a lot of other restaurants around the country, and that eventually led to Colonel Sanders opening his own restaurants.

Today, the Colonel's Kentucky Fried Chicken, with all its slick national promotion, and its new products that flash in the frying pan and die, still does most of its business in the rural South. Why? Well, it's surely not because Southern mamas can't fry chicken. Southern mamas can fry chicken just fine, thank you very much. But KFC is the next best thing to Mama's. It doesn't matter that the Colonel has gone on to that big kitchen in the sky. Or that KFC is owned by a corporation that owns a bunch of other restaurants. What matters is that there's a real Southern person behind that chicken, who had a recipe he wanted to share, so he loaded his pressure cooker in the trunk of his car and drove across America cooking up samples. Sure, that's salesmanship. But the Colonel wasn't selling only chicken. He was also selling the feeling that somebody's smiling Grandpa cared enough to cook up a delicious taste of home, just for us. He was selling hospitality.

Every part of the world has its history and culture, and in the American South, the history and culture are awash in hospitality. We know how to have a good time, and we prefer to have it served with good manners. People here still say, "Yes, sir," and "No, ma'am." We hold the door open for each other. We nod and smile in the grocery store as we talk to people we've never met, and almost anything from a birthday to a full moon can be a reason for a grill-out. At every turn we see family, community, and memories, wrapped up in the story of Southern food.

So isn't it amazing that an Okie like me, and

some other Southerners, created McDonald's world-famous Happy Meal while working in a Northern ad agency? It was a time when the nation was picking up its pace. Busy young married couples, working two jobs and taking their kids to soccer practice and dance lessons, were the best customers for a McDonald's fifteen cent burgers. Trouble was, back then, kids didn't like those burgers, so those little families didn't go to McDonald's. We simply printed some pictures and games on the packages, threw in a toy, called it the "Fun Meal," and pretty soon, kids started taking their parents to McDonald's. Why were we the ones who invented it? Because all over the country, fast-food joints were trying to sell more hamburgers, but our little team, who came from five Southern states, were thinking about the people who were going to eat those burgers. We gave them what they wanted, even when they didn't know themselves. We wrapped hospitality in fun.

Fast food got bigger and faster, with lower quality and less taste. American working families traded home and hospitality for ad slogans and sameness. Yet, when I moved back to the South, I found that none of that had changed the heart of Southern Cookin'. In Memphis, there was still a barbecue joint on every corner. The folks in Louisiana still salivated at the most casual mention of sucking crawdad heads. And I discovered a little café in Forsythe, Georgia that serves a Caesar salad with croutons made of grits. That's the kind of thing you don't see in Pittsburgh or Denver. By the same token, bagels with lox are on the menu at every restaurant in New Jersey, but they're impossible to find in south Mississippi. I asked myself, "How come folks around here eat grits, and folks up there don't?"

The answer is a story that began during our nation's Colonial and Revolutionary years, when the American South created a unique culture. Then it all fell, decimated by Civil War, and then in the last half of the 1800s, the culinary phoenix of the American South rose from the ashes of that war. The Southern way of living and eating was reborn, stronger, better-tasting, and even more different from the rest of the country than before. It was the product of good people, close to the earth, close to their faith, and close to each other. They were black and white and Native American, many of them devastatingly poor, learning to live together in new ways. Through hardship and suffering, with resourcefulness and creativity, they managed to feed their families. That broad and deep legacy, which became the culinary and cultural stew that is the South today, has only happened in one place and at one time in the history of mankind.

What's even more astonishing is that the world has grown more homogenized, and yet, the South retains its charm. We live in a nation of immigrants' descendants who are more mobile than ever before, in an increasingly global society, with digital access to virtually all the world's recipes. Relatively new items in the American diet, like tacos, avocados, and quinoa, appear regularly on Southern tables. People everywhere watch Southerners wrestle, rescue, and eat alligators on reality TV shows. Wisconsin hosts a world championship barbecue contest, and McDonald's offers a Southern Style Chicken Sandwich. Cake, Korn, and the Black-Eyed Peas are bands, and *Fried Green Tomatoes* is a movie. Yet, in a world of changes, while America enjoys French and Asian cuisine, San Francisco style, Southwestern, and Tex Mex, there's a tradition, a style, an ethos we call Southern Cookin', that endures and flourishes, much the way it did 150 years ago. There's no other local, state, or regional cuisine in America that is so pervasive, so entwined and identified with the history and lifestyle of a people, as Southern Cookin'.

Southern Cookin' isn't exactly a matter of where you cook it, and it's really not even a matter of where the recipes originated. Americans can find good barbecued ribs, fried okra, and grits on the menu all across the country. And the South certainly doesn't have a corner on church socials, pot luck dinners, good gravy, or good manners. What makes all the difference is the concentration and consistency of Southern-ness.

In this book, the "South" refers not only to the Deep South, along the Gulf Coast, but also the Carolinas, Virginia, West Virginia, Kentucky, and Tennessee. So is my home state of Oklahoma Southern? Consider the fact that our family's recipe for fried corn can be traced back five generations to southern Missouri, and before that, Tennessee, then North Carolina. During most of the 1800s, Oklahoma was Indian Territory, and then most of it was opened for others in great land runs. Many of the people who came were Southerners, and there's no better example of Oklahoma's cultural evolution than Elias Stanfield. He traveled all the way from Horse Cove, North Carolina, to try his luck in the land run of 1889, only to find that Oklahoma wasn't the Eden that the newspaper ads promised. How could he bring sweet Fanny McKinney, his half-Cherokee bride-to-be, out to that piece of parched red dirt? He abandoned the free land he had claimed, and went home to Fanny and the lush Carolina hills, where every year would bring plenty of game, grass for livestock, and a big vegetable garden. But they later moved to Arkansas, and their children, the grandchildren of Confederate veterans, ended up in Oklahoma. People kept coming from both North and South, blending their cultures

in a loose, wild, entrepreneurial land that was open to every modern invention and design that came along, and yet preserved family traditions. Though the landscape is decidedly western, the kitchen culture has always leaned toward the South. And because Oklahoma is largely rural and agricultural, it shares the South's deep love of the land, as well as its struggles with poverty.

What about Missouri? Is it Southern? Before the Civil War, it was a slave state, populated largely by Southerners, but with cosmopolitan French roots and a lot of German immigrants. Kansas City looked westward, and St. Louis was literally and figuratively in the middle of the Mississippi River between New Orleans' Creoles and the Great Lakes' Scandinavians. Kentucky, West Virginia, and Virginia have similar stories, being decidedly Southern, but bordering on the North. That entire area along the Mason-Dixon Line became a laboratory for blending cultures in the evolution of Southern Cookin'.

What about Texas? It was a cotton-producing slave state, and later, a favorite destination for Confederate veterans. It's rural, agricultural, and ready for anyone who wasn't afraid to make their own way, which are all solidly Southern characteristics. It has a unique culture because living there simply requires living like Texans live. The beef on Texas plates, as well as a full calendar of chili cook-offs, set it apart from the rest of the South. And yet, Texans eat fresh seafood, like everybody else along the Gulf Coast, their pecan pies compete with Georgia's best, they're proud of their barbecue, and their welcome mat is always out.

So if state borders don't distinguish Southern Cookin', what does? It's a tradition of ingredients and recipes that are rich in pork, cornbread, gravy, fried foods, and fresh-from-the-garden vegetables. But way beyond that, it's a celebration. It's gratitude in the harvest that begins anew every year as crops come in, and is appreciated with every spoonful of goodness, year-round. And it's the joy of making a lot out of a little. It's the everyday hospitality of, "We're glad you're here." It's a shout out the screen door to muddy, laughing children, "Ya'll wash up! Dinner's ready!"

If it sounds like we're blurring the lines between then and now, it's because that's what people do in the South. History is a compilation of close-up views that illuminate the big view. Little stories that explain big stories. It's the creek rising after spring rains that tell us why the town built a tall bridge there 200 years ago. It's the mint growing in a long-abandoned garden, whispering of hot tea to soften winter's icy grip. For the Southern cook, the best of what was, still is. To this day, the Southern table is equal parts heart and mind, stirred in with food, laughter, creativity, memory, love, and stories, all dished up on a 100-year-old, hand-painted platter that daddy's great aunt bought with money she made by taking in ironing. While we use microwaves and food processors, and while we've replaced our great grandmother's lard with olive oil, there's no way to replace the joy of following her hand-written recipes. Southern Cookin' is alive in remembered scenes of women in the kitchen wearing handmade aprons, men carving roasted wild turkeys, and big-eyed children giggling while they shuck the corn. It's alive in the family's favored dish, served with an old, familiar tale, which just happens to be the same tale that was told the last time that dish was served.

There's a place inside each of us that wants to know what it's like to walk into a barn and see the cow that gives us our milk. Or to stand at the end of a garden row, holding a basket of just-picked tomatoes with the sun on our shoulders. There are times when we wonder what it was like for our ancestors, sitting around a fire, sharing food they helped hunt, gather, and prepare. They were naïve scientists, experimenting, learning by doing, making their lives better. They knew the seasons of the moon and the best time to sow each crop. Plowing, planting, harvesting, butchering, canning peaches, and making apple butter, all turned into social occasions, times to get together and help each other, just like quiltings, barn raisings, and weddings. Life was marked by events, tied together with the sacred bonds of shared food and stories.

And we're not talking about just what Granny cooked. We're talking about her Granny, and hers. Southern Cookin' is rooted in simple dishes made in countless variations for generations. That's because our ancestors' hunger for food and family was fed the same way ours is fed. No matter how many imported spices we have in the pantry, or how complex the computer controls on our convection ovens, we still thrill at the sight and smell of butter drizzling into a slice of warm cornbread. We still delight in bacon and eggs sizzling in a handed-down cast iron skillet. Full-grown men still drool like babies when a serving spoon slides into a blackberry cobbler. For Southern cooks, the same care that goes into the entrée also goes into a bowl of mashed potatoes or a plate of fried squash, and our salads, breads, pickles, relishes, and jellies. We've got a dozen different scrumptious recipes for each one, and the main ingredient in all of them is love.

This book boils down a few hundred years of complex social and culinary history to pretty simple terms. There are big generalities and broad statements, and historians have a way of finding exceptions to broad statements. People in the South aren't all alike. Northerners and

A farm wife in Madison Co., AL, cans her peaches. (Courtesy of the Library of Congress)

Southerners aren't mutually exclusive groups. But in this case, it's not the exceptions that tell the story. It's the grand sweep of time, revealed in authentic, dramatic, funny, and heartwarming anecdotes. It's the little stories that make up the big story. All we're really doing is answering that question, "How come folks around here eat grits, and folks up there don't?"

I love the South. Sure, there are unseemly aspects to the history of the South, just like every other place. But when we love places, just like when we love people, we can't pick this and throw away that; if we're going to love them, we love the whole package. And that's how I love the South. Unashamedly, with a grin on my face and a half-eaten peach in my hand.

So this book isn't anti-Yankee. In fact, wherever you live in America, and whenever your ancestors came to these shores, you'll probably find something of your family's story here. After all, we're the first generation that's had the luxury of researching our ancestry. We have leisure time and computers, we can travel, and we can share digital information with people we've never met. So it's only natural to wonder how our ancestors lived, including what they ate. Maybe, after reading this book, you'll want to dig out an old recipe, cook something your grandmother loved to cook, plant a garden, can some vegetables, or make some jelly. Hopefully, you'll embrace *Grits to Glory* with a smile, a tear, and maybe new fondness for the amazing beauty of the human race.

This is folk history, not the way historians tell it, but the way the people tell it. All the people in *Grits to Glory* are real, though unfortunately, some of their names are lost in the mist of history. After all, some of these dishes were made and taught and passed down for generations before ever being written for the first time. The recipes and stories in this volume were gathered through years of very tasty research. They come from books, old magazines, journals, and government archives. From tramping through woods and along riverbanks, and from sitting beside campfires with hunters and fishermen. From smelling the rich earth in gardens large and small, following an old man who followed a plow that followed a mule, and from filling homemade baskets with fresh green beans, squash, and corn. From yellowed and stained recipes written on butcher paper and tucked between the pages of hundred-year-old cookbooks. And from countless interviews, sitting on porches and at kitchen tables, watching cooks at work, and listening to them talk about their food and their people. Because in the South, we can't talk about our food without talking about our people. That's our history: the little stories that make up the big story of *Grits to Glory*.

GRITS
TO
GLORY

All across the South, families know they can make a delicious meal out of whatever happens to be on hand.
(Courtesy of Library of Congress)

Chapter 1

Something from Nothing

It was 1866, only a year after the end of the Civil War. Hannah Higgins was a freed kitchen slave who, like many, stayed on after the war to work for her former owners, the Mason family of McDowell County, North Carolina. It was winter, the time of year when food was scarce, nothing was growing in the gardens, the food they'd stored back in the fall was dwindling, and wild game animals were sleeping away the cold months. Every winter was a struggle for poor rural families, and for several years it was desperately hard for everybody in the South. The marching troops, thundering horses, heavy wagons, and exploding shells had wiped out nearly every bit of livestock, crops, wild game, and wild-growing edibles for miles around. There was not a chicken or an egg on the Mason place. Hannah looked at the meager scraps in the pantry and wondered how she could pull them together into a meal that would feed everyone that evening.

About that time the oldest boy came walking up the road from town with a bundle under his arm, a package from Mrs. Mason's sister in Raleigh. She knew how hard it had been on the family farm, and had sent a few things to help. The kids gathered around, chattering in anticipation as Mrs. Mason reached into the box, and right there on top was a little white paper bag of gumdrop candy. Then she pulled out brown sugar, white sugar, flour, then peanuts and raisins.

Hannah was jumping for joy. "Now I know just what I can fix," she exclaimed, pouring a coffee cup full of the gumdrops and handing the bag back to Mrs. Mason. With a smile and a wink, she turned and gave the candy to the children, and they ran with it out the back door, squealing with the kind of joy that was rare in those difficult times. Hannah went to the root cellar and came back with a small basket of dried apples, then went to the pantry for a handful of walnuts and the cream of tartar, and then she pulled out her mixing bowl. She was working from memory, using an old recipe that called for butter, and she didn't have any butter, so she used lard. It called for sour milk, and she didn't have any milk, sweet or sour, so she added a little more lard. It called for eggs, but she didn't have any, so she had to leave them out.

The result was Hannah's Eggless Fruitcake. Everybody said it was the juiciest, tastiest fruitcake ever, and it was just the thing to boost the spirits of a family with a cupboard that was almost bare. In fact, in the wake of the war's destruction, it was one of many dishes created by resourceful cooks, who came up with dishes like "Kentucky One-Egg Cake," and the even more austere Eggless, Milkless, Butterless Cake.

But how did Hannah get to be so resourceful? Why was she still cooking for the white family that had once owned her, along

Sometimes the question of what to serve was answered by looking in the cupboard. This Arkansas root cellar, with its white-washed walls, serves as a pantry for familiar modern brands alongside home-canned goods, much as it did 110 years ago.

with her husband and children? At one time the Masons planted big, green fields and kept barns, sheds, and cellars full of delicious foods all year 'round, so how did they fall so low that they struggled to feed themselves?

First, Southerners had to get to a pinnacle that was high enough they could fall. And that's a story that started more than 200 years before, in the early 1600s, with shiploads of people landing on rocky shores while Indians watched, thought about killing every one of them, but then decided to wait and see where it all led. The Natives watched the pasty-faced foreigners plant some traditional European crops, leading up to a harvest that turned out to be no harvest at all. And when they were on the brink of starvation, the Indians fed them. So our nation was literally born in hospitality and shared food. That's an off-handed, gross

simplification of what happened, and the traditional image of starched pilgrims sharing a big meal with Indians around a big harvest table is mostly fiction. There were plenty of Indian hostilities, and plenty of attacks on Indians by hateful, racist, land-grabbing European immigrants. But people have always celebrated the harvest, usually accompanied by some form of expressing gratitude. And the history of America's pre-Colonial period is laced with anecdotes of peaceful meetings of Indians and European immigrants based around food. The Indians really did introduce the immigrants to corn and other crops, and really did help them learn to feed themselves in the New World.

Flash forward to the Donner Party, famous American cannibals, stranded in the hard winter snows of 1847, and starving until they sat down to a tasty meal of their best friends' hind quarters. All the while they were surrounded by Indians whose ancestors had lived through such snowy winters for centuries, and never once took a bite of a neighbor. The Donner bunch would have never made it in the South following the Civil War. They'd have whined, worried, and complained, while they chewed the last bit of Uncle Mike-jerky. Fortunately for the South, early Southerners were a line of Americans born in need, raised on charity, and nourished by hope. No matter what their circumstances, no matter what tragedies fell around their shoulders, they celebrated life, and could always find a way to live it to the fullest.

In the South, we still love old hymns that teach us to sing about our misery. We love the long, dusty, country road that's uphill both ways and never gives us rest. We love the foreboding swamps, where everything wants to kill us. The angry winter wind in our face, when we have nothing to wear but threadbare shirts. And the relentless sun that peels our skin while we toil at chores that are never done. Nobody suffers better than Southerners.

So while Hannah made her fruitcake, people were in the fields cooking corn cakes on the blades of their garden hoes. Women were scraping the last threads of meat from hog heads to make soup. Men who couldn't afford ammunition for their guns went out and caught turtles with their bare hands, and their children brought home baskets of berries and nuts. The kinfolks went over to Will Lewis's farm after services at Concord Baptist Church, in the Little Dixie region of Missouri. He'd get a big watermelon out of the patch, and they'd all enjoy a slice, letting the sweet, pink juice run down their fingers. Little Jaunita Maude Lewis walked to school every day with an egg sandwich in her lunch bucket. Then after the first frost, she didn't bother making a sandwich, but took the bucket anyway, and walked the long way through the woods, where she filled the bucket with sweet, orange persimmons. Then at lunch time she'd eat a few and trade the rest for somebody else's egg sandwich.

All across the South, families could sit down at a table of tasteless, leftover scraps, bow their heads, and say how grateful they were to have such good things to eat. For them it was never a question of how little they had. The question was only how they could make a fine meal, creating something from nothing. They lived that way knowing the Lord and the land would somehow give them everything they needed. They honestly believed that when things were at their worst, they were always going to get better.

Those families that were so poor after the Civil War raised up another generation who knew how to make a life for themselves. The Mason kids of McDowell County must have been forever shaped by seeing Hannah make

PORCH TALK

Nowadays, people joke that they pass fruitcakes around from family to family, re-gifting the same one every Christmas because it never spoils, and besides, they say, nobody likes fruitcake anyway. But fruitcake was once a Southern staple, partly because it could be made in so many varieties. It was essentially a moist cake with some combination— almost any combination—of fruit, nuts, and candy baked in. Usually, whiskey was cooked in, or poured over it, or both, which kept it fresh and moist. In a time when vegetables were hard to keep, and meat was hard to get, a fruitcake could be a meal in itself.

a memorable fruitcake on the day they didn't have enough in the pantry for a single good meal. When children of that generation grew up and married, they enjoyed a family garden, a few head of livestock, and fields that yielded two crops a year, so they could feed themselves and still have something to sell at the market down the road. They used their mothers' recipes and improved the ingredients. Then their children were able to go to the store and stock their pantries with familiar, consistent brands, and measure them more precisely every time they cooked. Then the next generation of children grew up, still cooking the same favorite dishes, still working from the same recipes, and Southern Cookin' just got better and better.

For decades, Southerners had to adapt to the changing availability of food, including times when there was hardly any. And people who are adaptable in one aspect of life tend to be adaptable in other aspects. They're survivors and optimists. Where others see problems, they see possibilities. So it was that Southern cooks formed a kaleidoscopic relationship with their ingredients and processes, with a deeply intuitive understanding of what it takes to make a delicious meal out of what's on hand. They worked with a palette of traditionally Southern ingredients, from bacon grease to okra, and traditionally Southern recipes, from stuffed and roasted pork tenderloin to pecan pie, always adapting to what was available. Like everything else in a Southerner's life, the meal on the table may not be perfect, but it's ours. We may not have everything we want, but we've got this. We'll make it delicious and while we're doing it we'll tell old stories, make new ones, and have a good time doing it.

Chapter 2

It Was Grand

History books feature pretty pictures of Revolutionary-era statesmen in handsome suits and Continental soldiers in crisp uniforms. Those heroes were real, but our nation was born in poverty and self-sufficient scrounging. We came from Europe as sharecroppers, day laborers, religious refugees, and convicts escaping punishment. Even if we had money and property in the old country, most of us had to start over when we got to the North American shores. In fact, as the pioneers moved west, they seemed destined to grow poorer before they could become richer. Immigrants first moved from the coast to the interior of Massachusetts and New York. Then it was all the way to western Pennsylvania and Ohio. A hundred years later they were going past the Mississippi River, and the move was still just about the same. When the family packed, they had to whittle their worldly possessions down to what they could fit into a couple of trunks on a riverboat, or what they could pack into a four-by-ten-foot covered wagon. They could carry cornmeal, flour, sugar, dried fruit, and some salt, but little other food. Some edibles were prone to spoil, and some containers were too heavy. Breakable jars were rarely taken. And they had few utensils, because those were heavy and expensive, and because hostile Indians liked to steal the metal ones. Some people had only one pot to cook in, which wasn't necessarily a bad thing, because it forced us to become a nation of experts at the one-pot meal, including stews, soups, and casseroles. In fact, that's what most people ate. Whatever they had on hand, that's what went into the soup. Some days it was thick and meaty, and some days it was luminescent corn broth with tiny, floating bits of reconstituted vegetables.

The Bible says Jesus promised that the poor would always be with us, but in America we promise the poor that they don't have to stay poor for long. Sure enough, in the seventy or so years between Bunker Hill and Fort Sumter, from the Revolutionary War to the Civil War, family fortunes improved. It's not that everybody was suddenly wealthy, but people devoted themselves to a quest for the niceties of life. They learned the joy of disposable income. Americans experienced the elation of making real wages, paying the rent, starting a business, and building or buying a house. They knew the pleasure of good-fitting, store-bought clothes, and tools, plows, and can openers that were manufactured in factories, instead of with their own hands.

After the Revolution, our food had a revolution of its own. As settlers arrived in Kentucky, Tennessee, and the Deep South, they planted more of what the Indians had already learned would grow well there, including big fields of corn. In the woods, they picked all kinds of berries, nuts, grapes, and greens to cook and make salads. When there was a wedding or holiday, resourceful people made sure there was plenty to eat, good wines, some music from a fiddle, banjo, and squeeze box, and plenty of room to dance. As time went by, more and more Americans began to experience a new kind of variety and abundance. It may not seem like much, compared with life in America today, but it was glorious when compared to the life American immigrants knew in Europe.

Back in England, Scotland, and Ireland, peasants ate bread and porridge, while only royalty ate venison. But when people got to America, there was no more royalty, and they found that deer were standing outside the back door, waiting to be shot. In fact, wild game was everywhere. So for many folks, meat became the center of nearly every meal for the first time. Every family had a milk cow named Bessie or Bossie, providing milk, cream, butter, and cheese. And embracing new ideas, technologies, and foods became an American ideal. President Thomas Jefferson was so impressed with pasta that he imported an Italian pasta making machine so he could serve macaroni and cheese at the White House.

The Americanization of macaroni illustrates how, in the early 1800s, America was becoming the melting pot it was destined to be, as people from various cultures brought their unique and often strange tastes with them. When a German family invited the neighbors over for a meal that included sauerbraten, even though the guests had never heard of it, they were going to give it a try. It was a fair trade-off, because most newly-Americanized Germans tasted mutton and crabs for the first time in America. The French immigrants were trying to get their neighbors to eat snails. Native Americans introduced the Europeans to pumpkins, and with their metal pans,

leavening, and sugar, the immigrants turned those pumpkins into fluffy pumpkin bread and even pumpkin pie.

Throughout America, rural and urban, there grew to be a sense that the family was going to be all right. In a community of poor people, nobody can afford to buy anything, which is just as well, because nobody has anything to sell. But when we became a nation of people with money, there was a ready market for everything all the time. If the folks on the farm needed money, they could sell a calf or a tea pot. If they had nothing to sell, they made something to sell. Dad could cobble together a chair or forge thirty feet of chain. Mother could give piano lessons or weave rags into rugs. The kids could gather buckets of blackberries. With farmers doing well financially, they got credit at the local store to buy seed and groceries, and everybody knew the loans would be repaid in the fall when the crops were sold.It was a new kind of rural life, in which anybody with a little land could make a living, acquire more land, and make a better living. We had been founded as a nation of promise, and indeed in rural America, even among the poorest families, there was no poverty without hope.

From the time one of our cave-dwelling ancestors first escaped a chilly rain to huddle beside a toasty campfire, one of the basic ideas of advancing civilization has always been that people can overcome Mother Nature. Coats could keep them warm, hats could shield them from the hot sun, nets could keep mosquitoes from biting, and improved oil lamps could extend work and socializing well after dark. In that same line of thinking, people wanted food kept cool in the hottest months of the year. Since ancient times, ice had been mined in great blocks from lakes and mountains, and stored in caves and masonry buildings. And so, in post-Revolutionary War America, ice houses did a booming business, with one of the benefits being that people everywhere discovered new varieties of freshwater and saltwater fish. Sturgeon, cod, crabs, clams, and salmon were common throughout New England, and were being shipped farther inland all the time. Oysters, which are found all along the Atlantic coast, led a double life, starting as a delicacy of the rich. Some elite thinkers even bought live oysters, and fed them milk to fatten them before eating. But then wealthier people moved on to more expensive and exotic fish, including the imports, leaving the oysters to the lower classes of folks. And what do Americans do when the market for their products dries up? They find another, bigger market. Sure enough, the oyster fishermen brought in even more oysters, and packers started putting them in wooden casks filled with ice, so they could be loaded on wagons and shipped away into the western Carolinas, Virginia, Kentucky, and the Deep South, as far as the melting ice would take them. Some homes served them on the shell, but almost everybody served them in oyster soup or oyster dumplings or oyster bake.

Although railroad box cars served pretty well as traveling ice boxes, there were limits to shipping food like oysters on ice. The train schedule was nothing like the schedules of today's buses and airplanes. Trains of that era generally ran every few days, at a blistering twenty miles per hour, while the ice in them was melting. More important, almost all of America's railroads were in the Northeast and along the Eastern Seaboard. It took decades for rails to reach over the mountains to the country's interior and the South. In fact, by the mid-1800s, some two-thirds of America's tracks were still in the Northern states. By 1860, for example, goods could be shipped by rail from the Virginia coast to Memphis,

Tennessee, but no farther. Following the Civil War there was a tremendous boom in rail line construction, but even then, rail service became a patchwork of major lines and short lines built by dozens of companies. For years, Monroe and New Orleans were the only places trains went in Louisiana. By about 1870, a traveler could take a train from Knoxville to St. Louis or Louisville, but the lines still didn't connect North Carolina to Knoxville.

The lack of rails meant that food, cookware, and other household goods could be shipped to a few major Southern cities on trains, but getting those supplies any father, to the folks in Jackson, Birmingham, and Valdosta, required combinations of river boats and wagons. That meant days spent unloading, loading, and loading again with the ice melting quickly on riverboats and in wagons, all of which didn't bode well for shipping oysters on ice. Plus, from the Colonial era on, there were hostile Indians, disease, and the general life-threatening difficulty of pioneering the great wilderness, all conspiring against commercial transportation, and making it very expensive. But this was, after all, the land of liberty, and by golly, there have always been Americans who were set on proving it. During those days of national expansion, freedom meant that the new nation's wealthiest people were happy to spend their money to get exotic foods to their tables, no matter where they lived, or how much ice, and how many trains, boats, and wagons it took. And that's how oysters regained favor among the well-to-do folks on plantations and family farms throughout rural America.

As wealthy Americans got wealthier, they hired cooks and built spacious kitchens for them. Once again, the widely-popular Thomas Jefferson set the standard. When newspapers reported that he had hired a personal chef who had studied in Paris, all the rich folks wanted a cook who'd been trained in Europe. Of course, those cooks with those big kitchens had to earn their pay, which meant coming up with an endless parade of recipes to amaze the boss, and that meant importing ingredients. Not just spices from the orient, which was a practice as old as Marco Polo. No, they also wanted seafood from far away oceans, champagne, bananas, coconuts, and especially pineapple. They imported foods like salsify, a European native root similar to parsnips, with a thick skin that has to be cut off before sautéing the flesh or adding it to soup. It was expensive, cooking it was labor-intensive, and it had almost no flavor, but people said it provided a favorite remembered taste of the old country, which was another way of saying it didn't matter what it cost. The best beer and wine were refined with imported isinglass, a gelatin made only from sturgeon swim bladders, so of course rich folks expected their beer to be brewed that way. Pineapple became such a pervasive symbol of wealth that it was adopted as a popular motif by artists, architects, and craftsmen of all kinds. The yellow and green, the crown of leaves, and the cross-hatch pattern adorned everything from stair rails and leaded glass windows to vegetable bowls, crystal wine glasses, and silver serving trays. Today it's said that the pineapple is a sign of hospitality. But it got that reputation because the folks who could afford pineapples were also wealthy enough to host parties in houses decorated with pineapples.

Somewhere along the way Americans developed a propensity for excess. If a little was good, more was better. If they could afford one thing, then they could afford the next thing. And for the millions of people newly enjoying the boom of capitalism, simply being able to afford something was a good enough reason to buy it. People who had been so poor that they never had enough to eat, found that they could earn a good living, which they spent on stocking their larders with lots of good food, including lots of meat, and then they found themselves gaining weight. Lots of it. Men got dressed in the morning and discovered that they could no longer fasten the bottom button of their vest around their great, overhanging bellies. Other men saw them on the street, noticed the unbuttoned button, and said to themselves, "He's so rich, he can eat a lot and get fat." Of course, they wanted people to say the same thing about them, so even the skinny guys started leaving that last button dangling, and it became a fashion that persists today.

Americans would one day indulge their taste for excess by killing almost every buffalo on the continent, selling the hides for European coats, and letting the meat rot away on the plains. They would almost wipe out the beaver to make hats, most of which were sold in England. They would cut the trees and sell them overseas, until timber ranked among the nation's top three exports. That kind of thinking was uniquely American, and it began in the post-Revolutionary era with people who found they could afford to import the world's most exotic foods. Like pineapples.

The steady increase in what was available and affordable began to create a sense of consumer entitlement. Americans were free, and the Constitution guaranteed it. They were free to pursue life, liberty, and pot bellies. They not only wanted to be able to choose their job and where they lived, but to eat whatever they wanted. They wanted to eat not only what was handy, and not only what they could raise themselves, but also what they could pay other people to raise for them. Canned goods made their appearance in the mid-1800s, making their way across the nation by wagon, then increasingly by train. Canned goods meant that people no longer had to limit their meals to what was currently growing outside the kitchen window or just down the road. Anybody with a little money to spend could eat peaches, beans, tomatoes, and cherries while blistering winds piled up January snows all around the house.

As American cities built better streets, sewers, and police forces, families had more reason to live in town, rather than on farms. In town, they could be closer to people like themselves, including people of their own ethnicity or nationality. In town, the men found good jobs at shops, factories, breweries, bakeries, dairies, and stores of all kinds. Their gardens, if they had them, were small, and got smaller as time went by. After all, if they didn't raise beans, they knew the store on the corner would have canned beans and everything else they needed. Besides, every day a farmer came down the street in a horse-drawn cart, selling milk, butter, and cheese. Another came along with a wagonload of meat, and another with fruits and vegetables. Ice cut from the lakes in the heart of winter was packed in straw in great warehouses, where more groceries could be kept fresher longer.

But as the cities grew larger and denser, they developed the sorts of problems that have always seemed to congregate in cities. In town, poor people had meager resources and little chance of bettering their position. They didn't have berries to pick. They didn't have wood, tools, or the skill to cobble together a chair. They had only their labor to sell. And the more laborers there were looking for work, the lower their wages tended to fall. And where were cities with the most poor people? In the North and East.

It was during those years that something began to grow. Something new and once again, distinctly American, the profound difference between North and South. Most of the people coming from Europe had been settling from New England south, into the Carolinas, and west into Pennsylvania, then in a steady stream, straddling the Alleghany and Appalachian Mountains like a lobster claw. Over the decades, it was as if our nation had poured this stream of hopeful immigrants and their descendants into a big American bowl and stirred them with a stick until they had everything in common, even with all their differences. We threw them into the fire of our war for independence, where they

PORCH TALK

Did Thomas Jefferson serve the same kind of macaroni and cheese that people enjoy today? Not quite. At that time pasta was considered to be quite elegant and exotic. It originated in China, then became central to Italian cuisine before being adopted in the rest of Europe, then America. It's one of the foods that became popular during the American cultural and economic explosion of the years between the Revolution and the Civil War, thanks largely to Jefferson's interest in it. His "macaroni" was actually what we call spaghetti, although many early American cooks broke it into shorter pieces.

Today Americans think of macaroni smothered in yellow cheese or drowning in tangy tomato sauce. But early recipes favored a distinctly white dish. After cooking, the macaroni was generally mixed with salt, pepper, milk, egg, and sometimes enough butter to float a passenger ship. Cheese was melted in, or grated on, or both. Crackers or toasted bread crumbs were added, and sometimes oysters, bacon, or chopped beef. Sometimes a stew was made of beef, garlic, ketchup, and currant jelly, and that was spread over the pasta in a bowl before baking briefly to blend the flavors.

were hardened and finished into something beautiful, rich-textured, and seething with life. Then after 200 years of slow growth, in thirty years, from 1830 to 1860, the American population doubled from seventeen million to over thirty million. And like some mad scientist's experiment, the Northern half of them settled into little squares.

There are lots of benefits to the squares dictated by life in American cities. Squares meant there were lots of jobs. Life in a square meant there was a regular income, and a weekly payroll meant the family could buy pretty well anything they needed, even if not everything they wanted. All things considered, there were more eating families than starving families in American cities of the 1800s.

Meanwhile, we gave up a lot to enjoy the urban life. We gave up the family. Maybe it was the family we left in Europe. Maybe the family we left on the farm. Maybe in another state. But even if they were only across town, we might rarely see them. We lost the little white church down the road. We lost the excitement of waking up to a different world every day, with the changing of seasons, chores, and crops, accompanied by the song of living, dying, and birthing people and animals. We traded that for sameness. The same pay for doing the same job and seeing the same scenery, day after day, and if somebody died or moved on, somebody moved in to take their place. We lost the sense of where our labors went and where our food came from. We were no longer eating the hog named Daisy that we raised in the backyard for the past two years. We were eating sausage made from someone else's hogs and shipped over from Pennsylvania.

In the city, there was no safety net of friends and neighbors. If daddy was out of a job, there was little he could do except look for another job. Mother was already working as hard as she could to keep the family clothed and fed. The tiny backyard garden didn't produce enough to feed the family year-around. They didn't have Bossy the milk cow. They knew that God helps them who help themselves, but if you don't have boots, you can't pull yourself up by your bootstraps. And hope, well, they began to see that was something for folks who could do something about it.

And that's why things were different in the South, where there were no squares, and hardly any roads. There were few steady paychecks, but there were more options, so even poor farmers tended to provide for themselves just fine. Communities grew stronger because everybody needed their neighbors. For example, James and Nancy Adair had a farm where they raised vegetables, hogs, and a lot of corn. James also had a steam engine connected to a wide canvas belt that turned a big, circular saw blade. He sawed the lumber for the church, his own barn, and his neighbors' houses. If there was enough timber on someone's property to build their new house or barn, James would hitch up his team of mules, haul the engine to the site, and saw the lumber right there. And when he wasn't sawing wood, he was working in his blacksmith shop or grinding corn at his mill, which was also powered by his steam engine. For all those services, he'd take cash or livestock in payment, thank you very much.

Their daughter Fanny married black-eyed Joe, a good man with a team of mules. He could turn a field faster and plow it straighter than anyone else in the neighborhood, so other farmers for miles around Hillsboro hired him to do their plowing. Fanny took in sewing and laundry, while their daughter Elida canned everything from peaches to tomato juice, using produce she raised in the garden with her husband Robert. He worked in a factory so they could afford to buy meat.

A Mississippi farmer and his white mule till the family garden. (Courtesy of the Library of Congress)

In the South, during the years before the Civil War, some farms grew into plantations, where slaves provided the labor. Everywhere that happened, social mobility virtually came to an end. The line between the wealthy and everybody else was hard to cross, and the rich got richer while the middle class and those below remained entrenched. Labor on the plantations became well-regulated and efficient, with the work carefully divided, and a hierarchy among slaves that ensured a smooth operation. Aristocratic owners drank fine wine while they talked about the details of how they ran their operations. Their overseers, men who managed the slave laborers, exchanged ideas, and slaves carried information from one farm to another. So, although there were few laws and no written rules of the slave-based commerce, there came to be standard procedures followed by most of the planters and most of the slaves, so that one plantation operated pretty much like another.

Since Colonial days, the Southern diet had been heavy in pork and corn, so it's not surprising that the slave diet included a lot of pork and corn. Both were hearty and easy to

Carnton Plantation, in Franklin, TN, is a grand icon of Southern grace, wealth, and charm before the Civil War. It once overlooked 1400 white-fenced acres of hay, oats, corn, wheat, and thoroughbred horses.

produce. Slaves lived in rows of cabins near the main house, or near an overseer's house. Some kept small personal gardens, where they grew vegetables to eat, and if they were lucky, a little extra for the children to sell. Some of them spent considerable time hunting and fishing, and some kept domestic animals, perhaps a mule and a milk cow. Some raised chickens for meat and eggs. Often, they sold their extra produce and eggs to the plantation owner for cash, or traded them for tobacco, molasses, sugar, and simple fabrics for sewing. In most

places, the law prevented slaves from learning to read and write, yet they were encouraged to organize Christian churches. It was in church that they developed a powerful sense of community, while exchanging information and ideas in a sort of secret society that gave them a place to remember the sweet taste of independence and a little power over their daily lives of hard labor.

Plantation chefs enjoyed well-stocked kitchens. Maybe the chef was a slave. Or maybe there was an entire staff of kitchen slaves

Mrs. R. W. Cleveland feeds the chickens on her farm in Elbert Co., GA. The little tree at the corner of the house is a peach. (Courtesy of the Library of Congress)

overseen by a chef from Europe. Dinner guests in Atlanta, hundreds of miles from the coast, would certainly have been impressed when their host served eels shipped all the way from New York, or crabs from Boston. Lemons were very popular, and planters found that some of the produce and spices from the Caribbean and South America would grow just fine in the South

Something else happened in the South that would prove to be critically important to the American menu. Native Americans had spent centuries learning the best ways to fish North American waters, along with the best ways to preserve and prepare their catches. They knew every plant in the woods and how to use it. Most of them lived on some combination of wild game and agriculture, planting gardens that featured corn, potatoes, peppers, and other crops that were new to the arriving Europeans. To farm Florida's sandy soils, white folks and their slaves had to adopt the Seminoles' techniques for raising crops and cattle. The culinary upshot of all this was a new Southern way of acquiring and preparing food, combining the best of European and Native American methods. Native Americans may have grown up learning to cook using baskets, earthenware, wooden utensils, and mud or stone ovens. But they were quick to adopt metal cookware, stoves, and modern utensils, just as the immigrants adopted their traditional knowledge of gardening, gathering, preserving, and cooking. The American menu became an evolving balance of meat, fish, seafood, vegetables, mushrooms, fruits, nuts, greens, and grains.

Americans were urban and rural, rich and poor, European, African American, and Native American. Gradually, we created a decided Northern thread and Southern thread to the American fabric that gave rise to the glory of distinctly Southern Cookin'. The rich folks in the South had money, time, and slave labor on their side. They could bring in the best ingredients, and then take as long as they wanted to develop recipes. If one batch of dumplings didn't turn out, the cooks would feed them to the dogs and change the recipe a little for the next batch. Poor folks in the South were inventive, resourceful, and diligent. If they didn't have food, they'd find it. If they didn't know how to fix it, their neighbors did. Lacking the refrigeration, transportation, and steady flow of imports that were enjoyed up north, Southerners worked hard at preserving each food as it came into season, so they enjoyed a more varied diet, one that was more in tune with nature, rather than trying to overcome nature. They couldn't see it at the time, but Southerners were giving birth to Southern Cookin'. By the mid-1800s, the South was the home of the tastiest, most inventive, most varied, most unusual, and most balanced diet in North America. It was abundant, and it was grand.

Chapter 3

War Interrupts Dinner

The Civil War started as the result of a complex series of events based on two very different philosophies about slavery and economics. It was a slow-igniting fire kindled by political and legal action, like the 1850 Missouri Compromise and the 1857 Dredd Scott decision. Then all that statesmanship blew up into scattered violence, like John Brown's bloody raids to free slaves along the Missouri-Kansas border, and the Confederate attack on Fort Sumter. And then came four years of massive armies grinding through devastating major battles. Before, during, and after all that, regardless of what started the war or kept it going, there was a distinctly Southern view of it among common citizens of the South. They regarded it as an illegal U.S. Army invasion that started in 1861, when most Southerners just wanted to be left alone. They didn't care a great deal about whether Kansas entered the Union as a free state or a slave state. They were poorly educated people who'd grown up with slavery, and generally, nobody had taught them that it was cruel and immoral. Family farmers had their hands full with things like getting up before dawn to milk the family cow. Big planters were busy making sure the plantation was producing a profit. But once the war started, Southerners couldn't avoid the conflict because it took place in their front yard.

The war was fought largely in Virginia, with major thrusts into Tennessee, Mississippi, Alabama, Georgia, and more sporadic jabs into surrounding states. For almost everyone in the North, their homes were safe, while people in the South didn't know whom to trust, or when the blue army might come exploding through their front door. There were divided loyalties in several states along the borders, including Virginia, Kentucky, Tennessee, Missouri, Kansas, and Arkansas. Families who declared their Confederate loyalty or whose sons and husbands were serving in gray were likely to be targets of fires, shootings, or beatings by soldiers or civilian Unionists. Federal troops were ordered to seize property of Southern sympathizers, and some parts of the Confederate states were under martial law for most of the war. On the other hand, there were Union-sympathetic families living in Southern territory too, and they had just as much to fear from Confederate troops, Southern guerillas, and neighbors who favored secession. Some Confederates needed only a rumor that a farmer had supplied mules to the boys in blue, or that a son had gone off to fight for the Union, and they would destroy the Unionist farm and kill the father while his wife and children watched. Southern veterans who'd seen their friends and neighbors blown to dust in the last battle, and guerillas who'd seen their homes burned, weren't inclined to listen to pleas or be charitable.

When it all began, there was a poetic asymmetry to the nation, with some eighty percent of the manufacturing and wheat production in the North, livestock and various crops being produced all across the young nation, and the South producing nearly all of the rice and cotton. Then just when it seemed that things were going so well, the Civil War came along and spoiled it all. Almost overnight, the able-bodied men were all gone. Over three million of them wore the uniforms of blue or gray, perhaps sixty percent of the nation's black and white males of military age. Less than half the Union soldiers were farmers, but in the South, two-thirds of the army came from family farms and producing plantations. Some were too old to enlist, over fifty, or too young, under eighteen, and some tried to stay out because they were holding a public office. But often those men who tried to stay home and keep out of the war for whatever reason, were forced to leave their homes and families because they'd been beaten or threatened by neighbors or raiders who opposed their political views. To stay meant endangering not only themselves, but their families as well.

With the men of the house gone, a woman alone couldn't possibly care for her children and do the housework as well as the farm work, so houses and entire farms fell to ruin. Then guerilla raiders or federal troops took everything of value, from mules to silver serving trays. They were sure to take the axes, hammers, saws, and metal kitchen utensils, because the armies needed the tools, and they needed any kind of metal to make cannons, ammunition, gun barrels, hinges, hitches, bits, buttons, and buckles. Soldiers, Confederates in particular, got so desperate for ammunition, they'd melt down almost anything made of lead to make bullets, and soldiers of both sides filled cannon shells with chain, nails, silverware, or anything else metal. They ripped siding from houses and barns and pews from churches to fuel their thousands of campfires.

In slave-owning families, the hard labor continued to get done for a while. But even there, it was the inexperienced woman of the house who had to supervise the field workers, talk to bankers, and decide what to plant, how much, and when. They had to direct the harvest, sell the crops, and take the grain to the miller down the road. They were often successful, but one mistake could mean epic failure for the farm. As the war wore on, slaves started walking away, and particularly in the Border States and Union-occupied areas, raiders returned to burn houses and barns. When a home was destroyed, the women and children had no choice but to leave the place, and if they were fortunate, move in with relatives. Everything was unsettled, and everybody, no matter where their loyalties lay, was afraid of what might happen next.

A Union medical officer, Charles B. Tompkins, wrote to his wife about seeing a beautiful plantation home robbed, then burned, by marauding Union soldiers, "The building cost $200,000. Five miles from this was a building which cost $125,000. In this was a one thousand-dollar piano. Everything was being destroyed." Miss Jourdan Woolfork, of Bowling Green, VA, wrote to a friend that most of the men in their neighborhood were gone, and almost everything was destroyed when the Union army passed through in 1865. They took all the family's food except one ham, all the clothing, except what was on their backs, most of the furniture, and all the livestock. Most of their slaves were gone too, which left the women with no way to cultivate crops or otherwise feed themselves. Yet, young Jourdan counted herself fortunate because some of their neighbors had "their houses burnt over their heads."

During the war, some of the finest public buildings in the South, and magnificent homes like this one, were destroyed by cannon shells and fire, and crops were trampled and burned.

Bromfield Ridley was an outspoken Confederate man and chancellor of the court in the county seat of Murfreesboro, TN. When Union forces occupied the state, they removed him and the other government officials from office. Then a couple of weeks later, they arrested some 200 known pro-Confederate men, so Ridley and the other former office holders left their homes to keep from being thrown into jail. As battles raged and armies maneuvered, the area changed from Confederate control to Union, back to Confederate, then Union again. It was during one of the federal occupations, after Ridley was gone that U.S. troops burned his family's magnificent home to the ground because four of the five Ridley men were in Confederate service, and the federal commander was sure their home was the hub of a spy ring. Not only was the family left homeless and the women forced to go live with friends, but their recently-emancipated slaves, who had always had someone to make decisions and tell them what to do, were left to their own devices. They had no tools, seed, or livestock with which to start over. They continued living in their same cabins, but always with the questions of how they would feed themselves, when they might be evicted, and where they could go if it happened.

The brutality peaked during General W. T. Sherman's infamous March to the Sea, when his troops lived off the land and burned everything they didn't use, to make sure the Rebels couldn't use it. Sherman's army generally marched in two columns, each from ten to thirty miles wide, mowing down everything for 200 miles along both fronts, across Georgia, from Atlanta to Savannah. His method of making war on civilians was unheard of, and the level of poverty, disgust, and demoralization it left among Southerners in its wake can't be exaggerated.

Before the war began, Kentucky was a slave state, but later joined the Union. It became a haven for guerillas, yet generally fared much better than Missouri, which was also a slave state, but with very few slaves. It was populated almost entirely by people from Virginia, Kentucky, and the Deep South. The state was deeply divided over both slavery and secession, and just to the west was free Kansas. Abolitionist Jayhawkers and Redlegs raided into Missouri, stealing slaves, setting them free, and killing their owners. Of course, Missourians saddled up and retaliated. Even those who owned no slaves would ride in defense of their neighbors, stealing their slaves back, and killing the Kansas free-staters who had taken them.

In 1861, when President Lincoln called for troops from every state, Missouri's legislature refused to align with either North or South. So Lincoln sent the U.S. Army to place it under martial law. The new military governor issued orders that the Army should seize anything that could be used by Confederates, which of course included livestock of every description. As a result, roaming Union patrols wreaked havoc, and guerillas ranged the countryside, taking anything they could use or sell to the armies.

By 1863, there was so much violence by guerillas on both sides, the governing Union general issued Order Number 11, saying nobody could live in several Missouri counties along the Kansas border. People simply had to pick up and move to a town, or move out. As for their crops, they had two options: turn them over to the army, or the army would burn them, a cruel and ironic tragedy, destroying all that food when so many civilians were hungry. For about three years, nobody lived in those border counties, and as armies and guerillas of both sides moved through, farmhouses, barns, and sheds, along with courthouses, schools, fine hotels, and stores, were all torched. It was a wasteland.

Across the South, scoundrels disguised as soldiers stole food and other property, from cotton bales to harnesses. Near Natchez, Mississippi, the entire corn crop was stolen from one plantation, while 600 hogs were taken from a neighbor. In 1863 the Confederate government directed that all the cotton along the Mississippi River had to be burned to keep it out of the hands of the advancing U.S. Army. That was cruel irony for the Southern army, facing a shortage of uniforms, and for the Confederate government, facing a failing economy.

Sally Fontaine Maury was as loyal to the Confederacy as the rest of her prominent Virginia family, which included cousin Mathew Fontaine Maury. He had resigned his commission as a commander in the U. S. Navy to serve the South. The Maury's suffered horribly through the war, and were happy to accept help from others in their family. Describing a package sent by a cousin in 1864, Sally wrote, "Hominy, peas & beans, onions, & red pepper, dried apples & walnuts for the children. We have not had dessert this Xmas though as we've not been able to get any

This view of the federal lines before the Battle of Nashville shows the devastation to the landscape everywhere the armies went. Horses ate the grass, and troops cut every tree for fortifications and fires. (Courtesy of the Library of Congress)

butter." In the winter of 1862, Nan Maury wrote from North Carolina to her Aunt Sally that they sold their horse and foal, they were trying to sell a cow, and a neighbor had hired away one of their slaves. Still, the family had "two barrels and a half of flour and about 200 pounds of bacon," she cheerily added, "We are not likely to starve." They had plenty of meat and bread, she said, unless the meat house and storeroom were robbed, and they were constantly afraid of that.

As the war went on and families got more desperate, in-laws moved in, and grandparents went to live with their kids. They sold off the plow, cream separator, and buggy. Then they sold the tools. Then the furniture and dishes. They made clothes from the curtains. Of course, everybody was in pretty much the same situation, so prices hit rock bottom, if a buyer could be found at all. Houses started falling apart because there was nobody to keep them up, and even if the family had money, there were no nails and lumber to buy. Things that were broken just stayed broken, and things that weren't broken, soon were.

There were few rail lines and few good roads in the South, which contributed to a poor distribution system for food. By far, most of

PORCH TALK

In spring of 1863, Thomas and Ann Elizabeth Lewis lived with their infant daughter on a little farm in the newly-created state of West Virginia, where they hoped they were safe from the war. But soon there were reports of a great Confederate cavalry raid into Ohio. Late one night, Thomas and Ann Elizabeth were awakened by their barking dogs when five men approached the house demanding food. Thomas knew they could force their way in, or even set the house afire if they wanted, so he had no choice but to let them in. They turned out to be retreating Confederate stragglers, and yet, their politics, or those of the Lewises, mattered less to them than the fact that they hadn't eaten in two days. While Thomas tried to convince them there was no food for them, Ann Elizabeth lit a lamp and silently slipped out the back door, descending the steps into their root cellar, where she scanned the paltry stock. They'd been eating fresh greens and peas from the garden, but nothing else was ripe yet. She brought up everything she could find to feed the intruders. As she would later write to her granddaughter, Virginia Collins Lewis, "The menu consisted of scraps (I called it) from a roast of pork left from dinner, stewed apples, a small dish of potatoes, also cold beans and some jelly, also preserves."

Ann Elizabeth's letter went on, "Well, what do you think we found next morning? Simply this; before they came to the door they had robbed our chicken roost of twenty-five or thirty of my frying chickens." The group's leader had politely insisted on paying for their meal as he left, and Ann Elizabeth wrote, "No wonder that man was so anxious to pay me for my trouble and what they ate too. The others who did not come in were making fires and cooking the stolen chickens."

the food was grown and consumed locally. With the dawn of war in 1861, one of the first military actions by the Union was a blockade of Southern ports, resulting in desperate food shortages and impossibly high prices in both rural areas and cities. In 1863, when bacon reached a dollar a pound, the women in Richmond, Atlanta, and other cities, rioted, breaking into stores and warehouses to steal the food their families desperately needed.

The great supply of Southern livestock was decimated. Chickens lay eggs for about four years, and then when they stop laying, they become fried chicken. Roosters live a long time, and as long as there's a rooster around the hens, baby chicks keep coming. But if the rooster dies, in the jaws of a weasel, for example, the family would run out of chickens, and in those days it was hard to find replacements. But the greatest threat to the family chicken coop, like everything else on the farm, was the marauding, starving armies, hundreds of thousands of men marching through the South.

Wild game had been a common part of virtually everyone's diet, and then it became even more central to Southerners' survival during the war, because by 1865 so much of the livestock had been sold, stolen, or eaten. And yet, relying on wild game was easier said than done because the men of the house usually did the hunting, and they were gone to war. Women, including those who'd never fired a gun, tried to learn how to shoot, hunt, and dress game. And with armies marching through, firing guns, and exploding cannon shells all over the place, and with wildlife habitat being destroyed, game was starting to get really, really scarce. People just had to do without meat more and more of the time. That had a profound and lasting positive impact on the Southern diet, as it became supremely important for people to have a long list of simple, inexpensive ways to fix a wide variety of vegetable dishes.

From the Border States southward, the countryside crawled with deserters and men avoiding the draft. If they settled down at home or took a job, they risked being found and arrested, so many turned to lives of crime. Later in the war, they were joined by wounded men and discharged veterans who were either on the way home or had no home to return to. All those men were hungry, and many were desperate, so they took and ate whatever they could find. It was a frightening time for families, and doubly so for those with no man of the house.

As the Confederacy declined, and the 13th Amendment freed the remaining slaves, a big plantation may have faced the loss of one hundred or so laborers. However, for a family that had been served by a couple of slaves on their little thirty acre family farm, the proportionate loss was just as great. There was no way for a woman and her children to do everything that had once been done by a husband, grown sons, hired hands, and slaves. The end of slavery's immoral reign was necessary and right, and the commercial system it supported was a false economy. But the change was won by horrific violence at the cost of the Southern social, political, and economic collapse.

Timing on any farm is critical, especially during spring rains. The ground can't be plowed if it's too wet, because the soil clumps, sticks, and pulls at the plow, and then dries into hard balls that are difficult for roots and water to penetrate. If farmers planted in that soil, some seeds would be left open to the air, and wouldn't sprout. Or they'd sprout and then their roots would dry out when it was impossible for them to push through the dense

clumps. So farmers had to be ready to plow and plant just when the soil was dry enough after one rain and before the next. If they planted turnips too late, they'd burn up in the summer sun. If the corn was put in too early, its roots would rot in the spring rains. A week early or a week late might make the difference in whether there was a crop at all. And clearly, timing was a lot easier for a plantation owner before the war when he had a lot of farmhands. A man working alone, or with the help of his wife and their young children, would find it impossible to get everything plowed and planted at exactly the right time. Even if they did, Mother Nature had to cooperate with the right balance of rain and sun, which was anything but certain.

It was a time when blacksmiths couldn't get iron and steel because it had all gone for railroads, bridges, and armaments. Harness and saddle makers couldn't get hides, because slaughter houses were closed. Wagon makers couldn't get wood, because the scavenging armies had burned all the trees, pillars, fence rails, and even siding. As a result, farm equipment continued falling apart. Plow shares would break, and there was nobody to make new ones. A buckle on a harness would break, and it had to be replaced with wire, which would soon rust and snap.

Virtually everything the South could raise or manufacture was consumed close to its source. Even after the war, when the Union blockades were lifted from Southern ports, there was little money to buy imports, and hardly anything to export. Southern factories lay in rubble. South Carolina once had a booming rice business, but the war shut it down, and that rice business was taken over by various other countries sending their rice to ports in the North. South Carolina never was able to recover its place as a producer of rice. In 1866 cotton prices went through the roof, simply because there was so little of it. Of course, the landowners scrambled to plant more cotton, and still, with no slaves, they couldn't produce nearly as much as was turned out in the years before the war. So cheaper foreign cotton was imported, and the next year more cotton was imported. Then there was a terrible drought that wiped out the entire American crop for two years, and those huge losses in cotton and rice income rippled throughout the Southern economy. Meanwhile, freed slaves who had once been forced to raise cotton for other people invested more of their time and energy into raising groceries for themselves. The once-booming economy of the south had been built on their backs, so without slavery, it collapsed. And all that was really a Southern phenomenon. Northern people didn't have many slaves when the war began. They didn't have big plantations to work. Northern civilians worked in stores and factories, so during the war they stayed busy making money, as the Northern economy flourished, thanks to the massive quantities of manufactured goods the Army consumed. People in the North were not only making rifles, pistols, sabers, and ammunition of all kinds, but also inventing new guns and new ammunition, besides continuing to turn out consumer goods. They made uniforms, wagons, and locomotives while they built new railroads. Some factories turned to the new process of canning food in tin cans, which were easily and quickly shipped to the Union Army. During the course of the war, though Confederate forces won many battles, the federals steadily overwhelmed the boys in gray with greater numbers, more and better equipment, shoes, blankets, and a far better diet. Their ports were open throughout the war, and they continued to import food of all kinds. Meanwhile, Southerners couldn't even buy a pineapple.

Chapter 4

The People and the Land

Today there are still a few fortunate Southern families who have been fed by the same land for generations, through good times and bad. In those sacred places, generations with the same blood in their veins have watched the same sun pierce the same horizon, the ageless rocks reflected in the same looking-glass lake, as crystal water courses through the same murmuring creek. And experiencing it is the only way to truly understand what it means to say, "This is our family farm."

When a Southern family was struggling, when everything looked the darkest, the last thing they gave up was the land. One family hands down the story of an ant colony that built a huge nest in their water well and ruined it. Those things just happen, they say. So they dug a new well on the other side of the house, and the water in that well turned out to have too much iron in it. The taste wasn't too bad, but it turned everything, including the laundry, yellow. Then they dug three more wells until they got a good one, because that's what families do; they maintain their faith that the land will sustain them.

Besides, in the years following the Civil War, there was no place to go. Even when Southern people were uprooted, most of them didn't go far. Couldn't they just move away into the city and find good-paying jobs? Hardly. A dozen of the biggest Confederate cities, including

Atlanta, Charleston, Columbia, and Richmond had been all but destroyed in the fighting. Southern roads, bridges, and railroad trestles were in ruins. The docks at ocean ports and riverfronts were decayed, and the riverboats that once served places like Vicksburg and New Orleans had all been captured by federal forces and burned or put into service on distant waterways. Levees were broken, irrigation systems were in disrepair, and ditches were filled in, so creeks and rivers changed their course, and there was flooding where there had never been floods before.

It might be expected that after the Civil War there would have been a great flight of African Americans from the Confederate states to the North. After all, the Northern states were the fountain of abolition and home of the Yankee soldiers who fought for it, while post-war racism continued to smolder in the South. Besides, there were jobs to be had with Northern factories, stores, ports, and railroads. But in fact, in the decades following the Civil War, few Southerners, black or white, moved north. They didn't know the towns, the people, or even the geography, so where would they go, and what would they do when they got there? And it's a good thing they didn't go, because living and working conditions in the Northern cities wasn't a panacea, Northern racism was strong, and Confederate veterans and widows weren't likely to find a warm welcome in the

Fresh, cool water still flows beneath this spring house. Ancient people drank here, then settlers, then Civil War troops, and finally a small town and two schools drew their water from the same spring.

North. So when people of any color left the South they were more likely to travel west, with its promises of wide open spaces and the glorious freedom of rugged individualism. There was land to be homesteaded, as well as the promise of jobs on farms, ranches, and railroads, and in mines, hotels, and stores, which were popping up all over the West, where there had been no towns at all.

But overwhelmingly, Southern people stayed, partly because the Southern Homestead Act of 1866 made almost five million acres of free land available to whites and African Americans alike. Even more important, they stayed because they had ties to the land. Whether they owned it, rented it, or squatted on it, they belonged to it. The American South, from the Atlantic coast to the Ozarks, from the Appalachians to the Gulf, was full of people who struggled and sacrificed to live where they lived. Everybody gave up something, endured something, to stay in their homeland and raise their families in the beautiful, nourishing South. When people fight that hard for something, they don't give it up easily. Southerners respond to adversity with creativity, not complaining. With hope, not whining. They don't give up because it's not their way.

It might seem that hard times and scarcity

might drive families apart. But rather, they proved to be the glue that holds good families together. Black folks and white folks alike were working so hard to feed themselves, they didn't dare go off and leave their loved ones to fight the battle without them. The common struggle united families, just as it bonded entire communities. It brought home the fathers and sons who had gone to war, and some of them had learned how to cook for themselves and others. Grandparents bonded more tightly with their children and grandchildren. Slaves who had been sold down the river came walking up the road. Some families had been on their land for two, three, or even four generations, so even if they lost everything else, they held onto the land. They knew that sooner or later they'd get a chance, just a little cash that would give them a foothold, and they could rebuild everything, literally from the ground up.

Some former slaves stayed on the same farms, working for the same families, with little change. Mammy Nancy Vestal, of Leiper's Fork, Tennessee, was born into slavery in 1835, and continued to cook for the Sparkman family until she died in 1903. Older African Americans in particular were happy to stay where they were. Even if they had health problems and were barely able to work, their former masters often let them stay on, and provided for their medical care. In many cases, taking care of black elders was the price farm owners had to pay to keep the younger members of black families on the farm. Former slaves would cut wood, do the milking, babysit, run errands, and manage the livestock breeding, feeding, and selling, plus raising crops, even if there weren't enough laborers to produce the huge yields that the plantations once turned out. They learned new skills, adopted new technologies, and in some cases made the giant farms work again by raising more livestock and planting new crops on ground that once produced only cotton. They might have been paid partly with cash and partly with shares of the crops, plus some milk, meat, and bread. A customary ration consisted of three or four pounds of pork and a peck of cornmeal, per person, per week. Everything else, like coffee, sugar, and flour, was part of their ration, but may have varied from week to week. Their clothing allowance was one outfit for summer and one for winter. It was subsistence wages, so keeping gardens, preserving their food, and cooking creatively were vital to their livelihood.

In the old days, before the war, every farmer could get credit to buy seed for planting, with his name and his farm as collateral. He could buy food and shoes for the children with credit at the local store, because everybody knew he'd pay off the bill when the crops were harvested in the fall. Or when the new-born livestock was sold in the summer. But not anymore. After the war, there were strangers running the stores. Heads of families walked into the bank or the store and were treated like strangers, because they were. There was no more credit on a handshake. To get a loan, a person needed assets, some sort of valuable collateral, and banks didn't want another hard-scrabble family farm for collateral. They already owned too much land because they had to foreclose on their previous loans. It was even hard for land owners who wanted to sell and move out, because during the war, there was nobody to buy their land. Most Southern banks were bankrupt. Then after the war, carpetbaggers, Northern speculators, and other opportunists were sweeping through the South like vultures, taking advantage of the desperate people and the battered real estate market, buying up land at a fraction of

A boy tills his sharecropper family's garden, using a new Kentucky-style hand cultivator provided by a government assistance program. (Courtesy of the Library of Congress)

its worth. A hungry family could look at a little cash in the hand of a smiling stranger, and see a path to clearing their debt at the bank, buying a mule and wagon, and getting a chance for a new start. Selling out to those opportunists was such an ultimate humiliation, a recipe for carpetbagger steak emerged. It wasn't steak at all, but a pitiful, creative way to fix the last remnants of meat, splitting and stuffing it with cornbread, mushrooms, onions, garlic, potatoes, rice, beans, peaches, dried apples, or any other vegetables and fruits that would make the meat look like more than it was, make it go farther, and keep the carpetbaggers from the door one more day.

Those speculators weren't buying Southern land to settle down and raise a family. In modern terms, they flipped it; they resold the land, often to absentee land owners, which were usually investment groups in distant cities. Those new owners sent managers to run their Southern holdings, and nobody in the whole bunch of them knew what to make of the former slaves. The Northerners often took a paternal attitude toward former slaves. Would they work or not? They once worked for no pay, so surely they would work for minimal pay. But who would supervise them? The supervisors sent in by the new generation of planters were men who'd been working in

Northern factories and other businesses. They had no experience managing big Southern farms. They didn't know what to expect from the former slaves, but did know how to manage Chinese and European immigrants in the Northern factories. So they loaded railroad cars and wagons with Northern laborers and shipped them south. An investor who owned a far-away Southern plantation he'd never seen could send his supervisor over to the Chinese neighborhood in Boston, or down to the New York docks where the Irish, Dutch, and Swiss were getting off the boats, and there he could enlist all the eager workers he wanted. Some supervisors even went to Europe and signed them up, with promises of work and the freedom of the New World, and put them on trains bound for the South. Many of the immigrant workers were craftsmen who had been among the world's greatest experts with machinery or clocks or furniture. They might have been genius engineers in bridge construction or mining. But when they came to America for the promise of opportunity, the opportunity they found was a chance to hoe potatoes and live in shanties. And they just didn't work out.

The main problem with the imported workers was that they weren't particularly good workers, especially in the sweltering heat of a Mississippi summer, or in a damp Arkansas rice field. Men from the foothills of the Alps had no experience with mosquitoes, snakes, and humidity that was higher than the temperature. They were accustomed to short work hours followed by long drinking hours. And when it came time for alcohol, they were sorely disappointed. They may have found home-brewed fruit beers, young wine, and moonshine from a mountain still, but there was certainly nothing like the dark, heavy beers of Europe.

They worked too fast and wore themselves out. Over the course of 200 years, people in the South had learned a pace that allowed them to work long hours on hot days, and the former slaves in particular had a rhythm that kept them toiling steadily from sunup to sundown. It may have appeared slow, or even lazy, to the newcomers, but it was a deliberate and productive pace proven to work in the South. Everywhere that former slaves, known as freedmen, were mixed in work crews with whites or immigrants of any color, the freedmen worked harder and smarter, and were more productive. In 1867, transplanted Northern foreman Will D. Gale wrote in a letter from a farm near Vicksburg, "I have never seen negroes more respectful, obedient, and industrious. And the amount of work has been more than even I anticipated." In 1875, Louisiana farmer George Montgomery impressed all his friends when he hired a Chinese cook, and paid him a whopping fifteen dollars a month. But soon, George fired him and hired a chef who had been a slave, who did a better job and made better use of the available food, for ten dollars a month.

Immigrant laborers generally ate at least twice as much as former slaves. For employers

PORCH TALK

The traveling Baptist preacher Asa Hamrick once said, "God could reach down here every morning and set your table, and then serve up fresh milk with bread with butter and peach preserves. But he don't. No, he reached down one time and gave us the land for our daily bread, and it's by working the land that our table gets set."

who provided meals as part of their pay, that was a huge problem. Many workers were getting "free" food for the first time, so of course they ate like every meal would be their last. Some had been poor peasants in Europe, with nothing but thin soups and porridges for workday meals, and they had never seen meat, eggs, and milk in such supply, or even in the same meal. But even if the planter wasn't providing food to his crew, the men had money to spend on food, and they were likely to gobble down to a big breakfast. Then they'd have a big lunch from their lunch pail, maybe beans and ham with cornbread and milk, while the Alabama sun was high in the sky. Then they'd work for an hour and collapse. The combination of overeating, indigestion, and heat would leave them sprawled out under a tree, sleepy, suffering from belly aches, or otherwise unable to work. Meanwhile, more efficient Southerners, black and white, went on being productive after a light midday meal, and waited to enjoy a big meal at the end of the day.

There was a special problem with the imported Chinese workers; they really liked being independent entrepreneurs. They'd talk in groups, in language their coworkers and foremen couldn't understand, and pretty soon, there they went, off to be fishermen. Or to open a laundry or other business that most men didn't want. Or to start their own vegetable farm, where they could produce more per acre on a little land than the big planters did on their sprawling acreage, have plenty to eat, and sell the rest.

Another problem was that the immigrant field hands didn't have any women. They belonged to work crews, ending each day exhausted, and did nothing else, so they had none of the richness of life that comes with a family. It's no wonder they longed for their wives, children, and the laughter, food, and customs they left behind. Besides, they kept hearing reports of the big cities, those in the North and East, as well as booming western places like St. Louis, Denver, and San Francisco. According to rumors and newspaper ads, the cities offered manufacturing jobs, including opportunities for craftsmen. There, a man could bring his wife and children from Europe to join him. There, he and his family would find a house, a school, and other families who shared their native language and culture. So in the end, most of the imported laborers simply left the South behind.

But above all, the real problem, the invisible problem, with imported labor was that they cared nothing for the place they were working. They only wanted work. Southerners not only loved the land, they were also bound to it, heart, soul, and mind. They were wrapped in enduring ties that were beyond their sight and understanding, but were more powerful than the economy, the banks, and even the war. The few imported workers who stayed to put down roots in the South were the ones who embraced, adapted, and contributed to the richness of the emerging Southern culture.

Through all the tribulations of war, profiteers, and scavengers who followed the war, along with shortages of almost everything from cash to nuts, some Southerners, both rich and poor, were able to make deals to stay on their land. Even among those who sold out, some were able to lease back a little corner of their farm. Or they found another place to make a sharecropping arrangement that allowed them to live on the land and work it for someone else, earning a percentage of the profits, or simply a share of the produce to feed their family. In the best sharecropping deals, they gradually earned a percentage of ownership in the land, or perhaps outright title to a corner, then an acre, and over time, more and more of it passed to them. It was hard. Brutally hard. And they went through times when they were even poorer than they knew they could be. But they did it because they loved the land. Their sweat, their blood, and their ancestors' bones were in it. They knew the secret places in the woods, the old familiar fields, hills, creeks, and home sites. They knew who lived over here, and what had happened over there. They knew their place was a place with a history that proved it could support life. It was a place where the mist hung around the shoulders of the hills, rising through the morning with the promise that each new day could be better.

Abraham Lincoln was wisely determined not to punish the South following the Civil War, but after he was assassinated in the last year of the war, his successor, Andrew Johnson, tried to implement his own philosophy. He was a Democrat, continually at odds with the Republican-controlled Congress over Reconstruction. He even opposed the 14th Amendment, giving citizenship to African-Americans. Then there was the lingering problem that during the war the federal government had put provisional state governments in place in Border States and occupied key Southern cities, as well as some entire Southern states. They had thrown out judges, governors, and other elected officials, and filled their seats with Republican federal appointees. And in the post-war years they worried about dismantling those imposed governments because replacing them would require new elections, and Congress didn't want to take a chance on Democrats winning those elections. It was very complicated. At that time, Confederate veterans were denied the vote, barred from public speaking or holding office, and couldn't even be buried in

the newly-created federal military cemeteries, even if they had at one time served in the U.S. Army. Meanwhile, newly-freed male slaves were given the vote and other rights of citizenship, and none of that sat well with some white Southerners. There were Jim Crow laws and the emergence of the Ku Klux Klan, which generated other groups bent on opposing and suppressing the Klan. To keep a lid on all that, the U.S. Army continued to occupy parts of some Confederate states for twelve more years, with orders to enforce emancipation laws, protect former slaves, disrupt white supremacy groups like the Klan, and to discourage any thoughts of reigniting the Rebel cause. And the worst part for the daily lives of Southern families, none of that was helping feed the people. That was up to the people, and they were oppressed, both in cities and on the farms, and limited on many fronts, finding it difficult to move, work, or start businesses.

Along with the army came a rash of failed federal programs that paraded through the South for twenty years. With the post-war federal presence continuing so strong, for so long, Southerners felt like they were living in an occupied country. Washington statesmen were talking about everybody getting along with each other and healing old wounds, but in practice, it was really a case of the playground bully making up his own rules.

During the second half of the 19th century, Southerners continued to share a variety of struggles, from poverty to lack of schools to political oppression, and yet as common as those struggles were, the South was not just one South. In its paternalism, the federal government failed to see that the Southern states were complex beyond what anyone could imagine. There were seaside towns and rural hamlets with vastly different strengths, weaknesses, and needs. Refugees huddled in cities like Atlanta, Little Rock, and Richmond, while many towns were simply gone, destroyed by war. Yankees, lots of Yankees, started moving into the border states of Virginia, Kentucky, and Missouri. Family farms were struggling to feed too many people, sprawling plantations were struggling to recover, and big acreages were being sold off in smaller and smaller pieces. From the east coast to Texas, from the Mason-Dixon Line to the Gulf, there were varied terrain, weather, and soil conditions, where innovative planters experimented with new crops and new planting methods. Where cotton had been grown year after year in the same places, depleting the soil, planters were dividing up the huge cotton fields and trying new crops in them for the first time in decades.

And yet, in the face of all that, the foundational institutions of their lives, family, land, and church, became even stronger, as the people underwent an amazing economic, social, and spiritual transformation. Everybody needed work, or a strong back to move something, or some nails for a barn, rails for a fence, or doctoring for a horse that was sick. One family needed help framing up a wall. Another needed blacksmithing. Some needed sewing, and some needed help with the laundry. Some had a sick relative who needed nursing and home remedies. People simply needed each other, and charity just naturally flows through southern blood, during good times and bad, as surely as spring water flows under the ice all winter.

They heard it from the pulpits and at their grandmother's knee. People are people, wherever you go, bless their hearts. They'd all been in needy shoes before, and maybe again. And if they had what somebody else needed, they'd share it. In spite of the paranoia and suspicion that lingered after the war, nobody is better than a Southerner at setting aside what divides them, and doing whatever needs to be done for whoever needs the doing done. Long before the Federal Emergency Management Agency, declarations of emergency, and low-interest disaster loans, Southerners were mobilizing to lift each other up after tornadoes, hurricanes, floods, and fires. When the twister blew through outside Success, Missouri, neighbors went over to check on the Tom Spurgeon family. It turned out they took a direct hit, so the neighbors helped Tom and his wife bury their precious eight-year-old daughter, then took them back to stay in their one-room log cabin. That way of living shone brightly during the crushing shortages of the Great Depression of the 1930s, which came along only about sixty-five years later, some three generations after the smoke cleared from the Civil War. Pearl Moon Stanfield, whose parents moved from Georgia to the Boston Mountains of Arkansas, recalls that her family never went hungry during the depression years because they canned and preserved and rationed. "It may not be what you wanted to eat, but there was always something," she remembers. "There were always people who had nothing, walking down along the road, and my daddy fed them and let them sleep on the porch." Those lessons, and that way of living, continues today, which continues to influence the optimistic, generous way Southerners cook.

One of the most important changes to emerge from the war was the rise of the Southern woman. It was the result of them discovering their own strength, along with the physical and emotional damage that had been done to Southern men. During and after the Civil War, lots of people were displaced, and families were torn apart. Men had been killed or missing in action, some deserted, some were demoralized and suffering from what we now know as posttraumatic stress syndrome. With army patrols moving throughout the South until the 1870s, some Southern veterans were afraid to go home. Some had no home to go to. With so many things different in Southern society, some men just couldn't seem to find a new place to start again, and they succumbed to that wanderlust that seems to be part of the fabric of America. The quest for something new. Just beyond the next hill. Farther from people, where independence was king. Maybe the gold and silver fields of the West would let a man go back home with plenty of money to help his family start again. For all those reasons and more, a fourth of those who went to war, some 250,000 men, never came home.

Among those who did return, many were wounded and disabled. About 30,000 of them had one or more limbs amputated, which often dictated their choice of where they could live, who they could live with, and what they could do for a living. It especially affected their ability to contribute to the daily work of keeping a home and family together. Even sound-bodied Southern men found it impossibly hard to get jobs. It was an era in which, as a group, they'd been defeated in war, left penniless and without property, stripped of their roles as provider and protector of their kin, and were essentially without personal power, their self-esteem shattered. In their frustration, they turned their anger on Republicans, the federal government, and the newly freed, independent, enterprising former slaves, and their own wives and children. A man who couldn't get a job could always find some liquor, get himself arrested, complain about his lot, and join a racist organization. But a woman with hungry babies to feed, livestock to tend, clothes to mend, and a garden to nurture, had no time for a man who couldn't or wouldn't pitch in to help. And for all their fierce loyalty to marriage and the sacred bonds of family, many a woman was forced to choose between her husband and her children, and the children won, leading to a rise in divorce and separations. That trend, along with the men who didn't come home from the war, left an unprecedented number of women living without husbands. For the first time in their lives, women became heads of their households, made decisions, and managed farms and businesses. In such times, many of them could turn to their parents, siblings, and other extended family, merging generations under a common roof, with all ages and genders doing their share for the common good. Though American women in general would continue to be oppressed by a white male-dominated culture for many more decades, the Southern woman stood taller and discovered more of her own power, thanks to the deprivations of the Civil War and its aftermath.

Southern pride got an unexpected shot in the arm when they started naming foods for American and Confederate heroes, remembering the noble aspects of their lost cause, and saluting the leaders under whose command Southern men suffered and perished. There was Robert E. Lee cake and General Forrest cake. Tyler Pudding Pie was a too-sweet dessert named for our tenth president, John Tyler, whose fourteen children loved sweets. General J. B. Gordon cake was named for the Virginia governor who had been with Lee at the Appomattox surrender. Confederates on Horseback was bacon-wrapped oysters or chicken livers served on toast with horseradish.

Perhaps the most telling story is that of Aunt Jule Ann, a former slave in the Warren family of Virginia. One night after the war, when the family had a dining table full of distinguished guests, and she didn't have all the ingredients she needed for dessert, she did her best to make a pie from what she had, which included plenty of sugar and eggs. Waltzing into the dining room, she announced that she was serving Jeff Davis pie, named for the Confederate President, a man she admired, although it was really the family she worked for who admired him. The guests were thoroughly impressed, and they all insisted on getting the recipe for the wonderful new pie, a simple mixture of sugar, a tiny bit of flour, cream, butter, and eggs. A week later, she served several Jeff Davis Pies to the delegates at a national church convention, but since the name Jeff Davis was decidedly unpopular in most of the country, she changed the name to Chess Pie. The convention delegates loved it and carried the recipe home, and that's the name it bears today, remaining one of the South's most popular desserts.

Like Aunt Jule Ann's pie, served in the land where tradition is lifeblood, every tradition came about as revolution. Somebody needed something new and found it. Maybe they saved up to buy it. Or traded their labor for it. Or maybe made it up out of spare parts. If it was good, they kept it, and if it wasn't so good, they made it better the next time. Through the hard, changing times, good people remembered the glory of the South, the warmth of family, and the joy of making and doing for themselves. They could look back on story after story of how Southerners had taken care of each other, before, during, and after the war. They never lost sight of the natural bounty of the land. And above all, they never lost hope.

Chapter 5

The Cupboard is Bare

The slaves had their own story, which was largely ignored until after the Civil War. Fortunately, that story was recalled and preserved when many former slaves were interviewed in the late 19th Century. Then in the 1930s, the Works Progress Administration commissioned journalists to interview more former slaves, who had by then dwindled to a few very old individuals, along with those who had been children in slave families. The result of the interviews was a sadly beautiful portrait of slave life, including both the hardship and the optimistic creativity of people struggling to feed themselves, keep their families together, and maintain their dignity, all seen through the lens of passing years.

By 1870, the labor force in the South was still mainly black, but things were changing in the Southern social world. The Negroes down the road were no longer known only by their first names, but were also proud of their last names, even if those names had been adopted from their previous masters. They worked for wages and they paid wages. They were on the roads, and they both worked and shopped in the stores. The black and white people weren't exactly getting together for afternoon tea, but folks were meeting folks where they never met them before, and relating in ways they'd never experienced. Former slaves were dealing in real estate and tending their own shops. They were the repository of all sorts of craftsmanship,

from brick-laying to horse shoeing, skills that a lot of non-slaves had forgotten. When a white man stopped at a black sharecropper's home and asked if he could work on their harvest for a few days, or muck out their stalls, or replace some fence rails, that was new for everybody.

It was the time of the Klan, the anti-Klan, and vigilante justice. State and local governments were being restored, and that included restoring law enforcement. Sheriffs and policemen had no training and were often elected or hired for their jobs just because they were military veterans. People were suspicious of the strangers moving into the vacant house down the road, whispering that no one knew what kind of evil they might be bringing with them. Why, they could even be Yankees, with their stiff manners and odd opinions. There were people in nice clothes riding on the roads in freshly-painted buggies, trying to buy land, sell insurance, and make all kinds of slick deals. Folks had to be careful. They didn't know who they could trust.

The new economy affected people of all colors. There was no middle class. People were rich or had nothing. Many of the old time big planters had a wealth of property, but no income. Their huge farms were expensive to maintain, so they were forced to join the ranks of the gainfully employed. Some had been lawyers, doctors, or politicians before they became plantation lords, so they simply hung

A Georgia mother and her children pick peas from their garden. (Courtesy of the Library of Congress.)

out a shingle and returned to those professions for supplemental income while they continued trying to rebuild the cash flow from planting. Some took jobs in shops or offices. They clerked or kept books. Wives who once lived in luxury turned to sewing, cleaning, midwifery, and crafts to bring in a little more money. Men and women taught school or traveled house to house giving music lessons. Some started new businesses and hired others.

If they knew the right people they might get a little private financing, perhaps a small loan from a friend. After all, there was still that upper crust of Southern society, wealthy folks who were willing to invest in craftsmen and shops. Some businessmen had come through the war in fair financial condition, with some assets, and were especially eager to invest in African American commerce. Generally, they chose to work with former slaves they knew to be dependable, hard workers. In Franklin, TN, Allen Nevils Crutcher Williams seized upon his emancipation in 1863. Even with the Civil War still raging, he used loans from his former owner to open a shoe store, which grew to become a general mercantile. Williams's sons worked with him, and as the store flourished, he bought real estate and resold it to other former slave families, helping several of them buy their first homes.

As important as school was, the schedule still had to work around family needs like harvest and hog-killing time. The rich folks had a history of starting all sorts of private schools for both boys and girls, from grade school to college, while public schools were scattered and poorly organized. Everybody knew the kids needed some education, and in fact, the post-war poverty in the South helped hasten public funding of school systems, simply because private schools couldn't fill the need. Black children had been barred from schools before the Civil War, so one of the earliest and most important social changes after the war was the opening of black schools all over the country, many of them started by organizations like the Freedmen's Bureau. Slowly, the new public school systems began to include separate schools for African Americans. Schools wouldn't begin to be integrated for another

One of the many ways Southern glory was reborn after the Civil War was breeding horses, including world-class racing thoroughbreds. Harlinsdale Farms, founded in 1933, was key in the development of the Tennessee Walking Horse. (Courtesy of the Tennessee State Library.)

hundred years, but at least the thousands of former slave children were getting some education. The changes reached all the way to the college level. Renowned Fisk University in Nashville, founded in 1866, was one of many federally-funded college campuses especially for African Americans, and like several others, today it's fully integrated.

Black and white people were learning something else. Some folks were new to physical labor, and were developing calluses for the first time. Other folks were new to management and had to learn how to coax, encourage, and lead others, instead of doing it all themselves. What's more, all those people in all those new roles had to hammer out their work schedules. In 1882, one farmer wrote that it was necessary to issue strict orders to keep the black hands from taking the team to plow before sunup. It was a big change, because as slaves, they'd always been in the fields well before the break of day. But there was no sense in doing that if the other workers, including the farmer himself, weren't going to show up until after a good breakfast.

Weekends had been more or less standardized in the work schedules of the old plantation field hands. Everyone rested on Sunday, except those slaves with kitchen and house duties. Working on Sunday was frowned upon, partly because of tradition, partly because the preacher said not to, and partly because hardworking people simply needed to rest. Some were also off all day or half a day on Saturday. So after emancipation, lots of employers expected that the African Americans would be thrilled to work for wages on Saturday. But in most places, there was no amount of money, and no accusation of laziness, that could move a former slave to take Saturday work. They wanted the extra rest that Saturday offered, but more important, that was

their day to work on their own house, tend their own garden, care for their own livestock, and be with their families. As a result, employers found that white employees would work on Saturday, but not black employees.

Then there was the paternalism of antebellum plantations. It had to change from the way it was before emancipation, but nobody knew exactly how to change it. In the old days, a slave who was too old to work might be kept on the farm and nursed until the end of life, even when he became too feeble to be a productive worker. When a slave needed a doctor, the owner paid the bill. A slave who had been crippled in an accident might be kept on the place peeling onions and potatoes for the kitchen. The sick were nursed, and even orphans were taken in, sometimes to be raised by slave families, and sometimes by the masters. So starting in the middle 1860s, everybody had to decide how they were going to handle those situations. Black people were learning to stand on their own feet, and whites were often unsure whether to help or not. In Cumberland County, Tennessee, Alexander and Lydia Hays wanted to take in Jacob, the son of their cook, after she died. The boy's father was long gone, but the cook, Jacob's mother, had other relatives, and the Hays family didn't want to offend the boy's maternal kinfolks if they wanted to take him in. Finally, everybody agreed that little Jacob should grow up in the white home, where he'd be tutored along with the Hays children, and would always be assured of a job. It was a story that was repeated countless times throughout the South. In 1869, one Mississippi planter was still supporting two blind freedmen. They couldn't contribute any meaningful work at all, and yet their former owner refused to turn them out.

So all that was happening on the social

and business side of life, while somebody was in the kitchen trying to put together two or three meals every day. It was so difficult that sometimes the best they could do was to mush up cornbread in buttermilk. With salt and pepper, it became a poor people's treat. One of Sally Maury's letters tells of fixing a meal in which she wanted to use dried apples to make apple dumplings. She was sad because she had to settle for serving the apples stewed, because there wasn't enough flour to make the dumplings. Coffee was a luxury, so some folks developed a taste for a hot drink made from charred corn. They also substituted parched barley, wheat, or even carrots. When they had a little coffee, they stretched it by adding dried peas, and some people liked it better that way. Or at least they smiled and said they did. Shortages just led to opportunities, not to mention good attitudes.

Anybody who's been poor knows that starch is the surest way to fill the family's bellies. That means rice, potatoes, rice, corn, rice, and more rice. A heaping bowl of rice and beans is packed with nutrients. It's got protein, fiber, vitamins, carbohydrates, and most important, starch. But if there are no beans, the rice is still fine. Sometimes a hungry family just needed to find something, anything, to put in the rice for a little flavor, and make it different from yesterday's rice. In fact, that single fact, the cheapness of rice during the Reconstruction Era, was the spark that lit the fire under Southern Cookin'. Most of the rice during that era was imported, and while that was bad for the Southern economy, it sure kept a lot of folks fed.

Southern cooks had watched Granny make the same dishes time after time. They'd heard their elders describe how they dressed the meat and made the meals. They'd seen all the versions and substitutions for different

ingredients when the cupboard was bare. And sooner or later, they had to recreate it when Granny and Grandpa were no longer around, proving over and over the power of learning by experience. Then there was the post-mortem, when they analyzed why the dish turned out a little different than last time. Did they leave something out or add a little too much? Did they stir the batter too long or was the oven too hot? And that's how they made it better the next time.

They retold the old story about how Grandpa cut that mess of fish into filets. Or how Daddy smoked the hams. They remembered how Mama put up the preserves, and how good they were on a biscuit when the pot-bellied

PORCH TALK
Hoe Cakes

One 1870s recipe called "Cheap Recipe for Batter Cakes" described blending a pint of sour milk, a teaspoon of baking soda, a tablespoon of flour, and enough cornmeal to "make a good batter." Then "bake on a hoe." Those were hoe cakes, a fascinating meal that originated in the slave era. A cook would mix up a big bowl of cornmeal, water, salt if they had it, and an egg if there was one. Flour or milk or both. Maybe a little molasses. The cook would carry that bowl of batter out to the edge of the field and build a little fire. Then the workers would come in, and one of them would brush the dirt off his hoe and hold it in the fire. When it was good and hot, the cook would put a dollop of batter on there, and in a couple of minutes, it was cooked into a hoe cake, a tasty, energy-packed snack. In fact, it was so good and easy, many cooks in the South started keeping a hoe head without the handle in the kitchen, a slave solution that worked for everybody.

wood-burning stove was the home's only heat in the gray gloom of a frigid winter. They kept remembering, kept telling stories, and kept cooking. If Cousin Janet didn't remember how to do it, Cousin Beverly did. And the result was not only about this ingredient or that, or about one meal or another, but about a new Southern Cookin', blending resourcefulness, memories, anecdotes, love, and creativity. It was free-form and flexible, and that's why it continued to get tastier.

Lizzie Morris Tingley, a woman who spent the first ten years of her marriage moving from one home to another in a covered wagon, never used a written recipe. She told her grandchildren, "It was all a pinch of this and a dash of that." In her era, being a good cook didn't necessarily mean you could read and write, which was only one of the reasons that hardly anybody had a cookbook. In the first half of the 1800s, books of any kind were rare and precious. If a family was fortunate enough to have a few books on the living room shelf, they were usually fiction, poetry, and essays. And besides, Southern Cookin' grew up in a time when boys got only a little education and girls got even less. So if a cook did write a recipe, it was usually without the kind of measurements we use today. They'd use descriptions like, "Butter the size of a walnut." In fact, it wouldn't have helped much to specify teaspoons and such, because poor folks didn't own measuring cups and spoons. Writing a recipe would have been like a wheelwright pausing to jot down each step in making a wagon wheel; the time was better spent showing an apprentice how to do it, an apprentice who would teach others as time went by. Recipes were alive in people.

Women of that era had no more important job than cooking, so they memorized the dishes as they made them over and over.

Over the years, their children and their children would refine and modernize the recipes, and write them down with increasing detail. But it's amazing that Southern Cookin' was ever passed down as it was, when so much of it was done on the run. Granny measured the cornmeal and fed the baby. She cracked the eggs and scrubbed the floor. And when a woman that busy taught Lil Bit how to make mountain cake, she wouldn't point to a list of instructions; she'd expect the child to watch and remember. All the Lil Bits learned by watching and remembering the same dishes being prepared over and over again.

Milly Martin was born in Louisiana. Her mother died when she was small, and her father abandoned her, so she went to work as a housekeeper in various homes from the age of ten, working for her room and board. She learned to cook by watching a series of other cooks. And she ended up in Southeast Texas, where she married into the Simpson family, and became famous around the coast for her smothered crabs.

Young Paula Jean London's parents left her with Grandma Stella Marsden almost every weekend, and those were always opportunities to help Stella make luscious things like her Coca-Cola cake with its maple-tasting brown sugar icing. Although Coca-Cola Cake's Southern origins are obscure, it certainly began a long time ago. Coke was invented in Columbus, GA, by druggist John Pemberton in 1886, and was soon adopted by cooks in place of baking powder or soda to help leaven their baked goods. The carbonation in the soda provided leavening, and of course the drink added a tangy sweetness. As time went by, Paula Jean and others in the family would write Grandma Stella Marsden's recipes, so most of Stella's best have been preserved, including her Coca Cola Cake. And yet, her

Lizzie Tingley takes time from cooking, still wearing her apron, to have her picture taken with her husband Charlie. It's said that she was never seen without an apron on, except to go to church. (Courtesy of Patty Tingley Sisco)

amazing brown sugar icing remains a mystery. Many icing recipes come close, but to this day, the family swears that nobody can quite duplicate the combination of Grandma Stella's amazing cake with its thick, golden-brown frosting.

When it came to cooking without written recipes, all slaves had always done that, because before emancipation it was against the law for them to learn to read and write. Besides, they couldn't do much meal planning, because they once depended on rations and the scraps from their owner's kitchen. They got the fat meat, back meat, and pigs' feet, which helps explain why today's Southern menu includes so many varieties of beef ribs, pork ribs, short ribs, baby back ribs, country style, and flank ribs. Like widows in the book of Ruth, they got the beans that were missed in the harvest, and the wormy corn left on the stalk. They got the leftovers that house slaves brought back to the cabin after the white folks had eaten. When the pretty green parts of the lettuce had been eaten, they put what was left into a pot with a little meal and "butter the size of a walnut," and had lettuce soup. They spent generations learning to make do. They kept a pot on the hearth, and whatever they had was thrown into the pot. They might not have had enough meat for a main course, but it only took a little meat to make broth. A handful of greens that wouldn't feed the family would still add flavor and nutrition to the soup. In their experience, everything was in short supply at one time or another, and sometimes it was all in short supply at the same time. So when times got tough, former slaves and their children had plenty of experience to fall back on, making them adaptable and innovative in the kitchen.

One of the pivotal additions to American cuisine came over on the slaving ships many decades before. Most African slaves were rounded up in cruel, violent raids, and driven onto ships like cattle, without even a chance to say goodbye to their families. But in the midst of that evil, some slave somewhere pointed out to some open-minded white person that Americans could benefit from the foods the slaves knew so well how to cultivate back in Africa. Then some traders gave the next boatloads of captives a chance to bring with them seeds of collard greens, peas, okra, sweet potatoes, watermelon, and sesame. That's how those foods started becoming favorites in the South, and why they were a vital part of the revival of Southern Cookin', while they never gained the same kind of popularity in other parts of the country. Okra, in particular, thrives on the late August Southern sun, and lends itself to frying, soups, and the classic Southern creation, gumbo.

There are as many variations to gumbo as there are cooks. It's both Creole and Cajun, the Cajun versions generally being more heavily seasoned, but not necessarily spicier. Though some old recipes were made without okra, most people now consider it to be essential. In fact, the name gumbo is believed to be a mispronunciation of African or Native American words for okra.

Gumbo may include every kind of vegetable, from tomatoes to sweet and hot peppers, along with chicken, sausage, shellfish, or any other combination of meats that are available, and it's all served on a bed of rice. If oysters are available, they go into the pot, along with the water they were packed in. On the other hand, the rice is "boiled dry," meaning it's going to have a soup stock ladled onto it, and it shouldn't have enough water left to dilute the mixture. It also gets a little ground sassafras leaves, known as file'. Jambalaya is similar, but is made in one pot with the rice cooked in. And those two dishes formed the foundation of

Creole and Cajun cooking, as they spread from Louisiana and the Gulf Coast because they were so well-suited to the Southern palate and the Southern pantry.

The heart of all Louisiana cuisine is the roux, a sort of gravy, and though a recipe needs only a couple of spoons full, it's enough to make all the difference in a great gumbo. The roux is made by melting a tablespoon of lard over a pretty hot fire, then stirring in a tablespoon of flour, and stirring constantly until it's dark brown and thick. It happens quickly. In fact, the hot skillet almost has to be removed from the fire as soon as the flour goes in. As they say, "Great cooks make great roux."

For over one hundred years, African Americans helped give the South a face of joy and hope. They came from tribal cultures with communal standards of shared work, and somehow, through slavery, emancipation, Reconstruction, and into the twentieth century, those standards survived. They brought farming skills from Africa, along with relentless persistence that characterized slave families as they fed themselves and the families they served, in some of the hardest imaginable circumstances. The culture they created proved to be a bedrock that bridged their changing world from slavery to freedom and beyond. They brightened their nights with dancing and singing, their banjos and fiddles resounding across the fields. They raised the roofs of their churches with raucous, soulful spirituals sung to the ringing of tambourines. Whatever their trials, the songs they shared united them as a people and rejuvenated them as individuals. Food, music, family, and community were simply inseparable.

All of that went into the stewpot of history, helping to create the taste and color of Southern Cookin'. It was different folks with different experiences, but sharing some of the same struggles, opportunities, and hope. Somehow, separately and together, over smoking stoves in tumble-down shacks, and in spotless kitchens of white-washed mansions, they evolved a new way to live and a gloriously Southern way to cook.

During that time the Southern brain evolved a direct biological link between God and food. Cooks in the Southern tradition will still say, "It's just as easy to cook for forty as it is for four," and they learned that by cooking for the church congregation. From the preacher's standpoint, that's one way to keep the flock in the fold: feed them. Some churches have summer singings, accompanied by watermelon

PORCH TALK

Almost every cook has been in the middle of making something and realized that they don't have one of the ingredients. If they intend to bake an apple pie and discover that they have no apples, that's pretty well the end of it. But sometimes they can make substitutions, and part of being a great cook is knowing what's on hand and how to use it.

For allspice, substitute half cinnamon and half ground cloves.

For a teaspoon of baking powder, substitute half baking soda and half cream of tartar, or a little baking soda in a half cup of buttermilk.

For a cup of buttermilk, or sour milk, substitute a cup of sweet milk plus a tablespoon of lemon juice or vinegar, and the milk will sour. Mothers often took the opportunity to mention that people are much the same: all it takes is a little temptation, a little greed, or a little dishonesty, and we're soured.

For a cup of flour, substitute one and a half cups of bread crumbs.

And every great cook knows that the one ingredient in every recipe that has no substitute is love.

or hand-cranked ice cream, and anything from a revival to the Fourth of July can be a reason for a full meal. The Catholics call it a covered dish supper. Down at the Antioch Baptist Church it's dinner on the ground, which is short for staying after the service to share a big pot-luck at the church grounds. Today folks might be sitting around big plastic tables in the air-conditioned Fellowship Hall and spooning up buttered carrots from electric chafing dishes, but 150 years ago, folks were picnicking outside under the trees on sawmill planks set up on barrels. Kids played and threw rocks in the creek, just like they do today. Conversations turned to who died, who's getting married, who's expecting a baby, and who was adding a room onto the house, just like today. One hot topic over a plate of grilled chicken, potato salad, and sliced tomatoes, has always been transportation, whether that means comparing horses' teeth, taking the train to the big city, or getting the best gas mileage. And now, just like back then, when everybody has eaten their fill and is just nodding off for a little nap, the preacher herds them back inside for more singing and preaching that doesn't break up sometimes until well after dark.

Some of the South's best meals are eaten at those church socials. Southern cooks aren't the kind of people who snap their fingers, remembering at the last minute that there's a dinner at the church, then stop on the way and pick up a store-bought cake. No, they plan for it. Why? Because they want to please the people they love. And because they know their friends will bring their best, and they want to honor them with their best. Anybody who has ever raised cucumbers and made them into pickles knows how much work went into the pickles, which can usually be found in at least a half-dozen varieties from sugar-sweet to pucker-up sour. Smiles, laughs, and animated conversation swirl around produce fresh from the garden. Applesauce and stewed tomatoes. Breads, cobblers, and pies. Meatloaf and country ham. Southern food teaches us to be thankful and say so. It teaches us to remember that a full table is a blessing, because the tables of our families haven't always been so full. When they're not full, we make it through by having faith that they will be again. And when they fill up, by golly, we celebrate. We say grace and pass the gravy.

All people are descended from a time when the necessities of life—parents, siblings, friends, God, the land, weather, and food— were all close at hand, in the place where we were born, lived, and died. At those tables we learned how to love people and love life, when we looked up from a delicious meal and saw the faces of dear ones who prepared it. And with that comes faith in a providing Creator, the cycle of the seasons, and the vast variety and abundance of the earth. Nowadays, a lot of people live alone in apartments in huge, noisy cities, isolated by distance, busy schedules, crowds, and strange, unchanging concrete landscapes. But even there, a little Southern Cookin', simply inviting a friend to share a roast and potatoes, can conjure up an old, familiar vision of who we are, where we came from, our faith, our family, our home, and special meals that will never be forgotten.

Chapter 6

Native Sons and Daughters

Three major rivers flowed into modern Southern Cookin'. Former slaves did their part. Poor folks of all kinds did their part. And Native Americans had some unique approaches to feeding their hungry families. Sadly, their contributions have largely gone unappreciated, simply because in many cases, nobody knew the Indians were Indians. Some of the Indians didn't even know.

Rosie Davidson was about a wide as she was short, an apple-faced woman with an apple figure. All her brothers and sisters told their children, and she told her children, including those who were born in Missouri as late as the 1920s, never to tell anybody that they were part Indian, because the government would take their land away. It didn't matter that Rosie and Allie Davidson never owned a piece of land in their lives. The Indians had been rounded up and moved on the Trail of Tears, and the Davidsons lived with the inherited fear that it could happen again.

In Rosie's case, it was hard to hide her Cherokee and Sioux blood, because everybody said the older she got, "the more Indian she got." If she and Allie needed something to eat, she'd take her .22 rifle, walk out the back door, and pretty soon she'd come back with a squirrel, rabbit, or muskrat. She was always bringing in greens and roots and mushrooms nobody knew the names of. She and Allie never had any money to speak of, but neither they nor a guest in their home went hungry.

They were typical Native Americans living among white people, who generally didn't announce, "Hey, I'm an Indian." They were busy going about their lives like everyone else. Some German descendants spoke Deutsch in their homes, and some Jews kept their holidays, in the same way some Indians spoke their native language and kept their traditions, modestly, at home. Then in public, they simply blended in.

For untold years before the Europeans came and started pushing the tribes around, many tribes migrated to various temporary villages, sometimes retracing the same routes every year, covering the same territory for hundreds of years in some cases. There were no state lines back then. No city limits signs. People didn't fence their yards. There were no Indian surveyors. And within tribes and clans the people shared their land in common. Though there were hundreds of American tribes, some of those best known today lived in the South. Very generally, the Cherokee ranged from modern-day Virginia into the Carolinas, and the Muskogee-Creek and Seminole, lived farther south. The Choctaw were in Alabama, Missouri was home to the Osage, and Shawnee and Chickasaw lived in Kentucky and Tennessee.

The Native North American population was at least two million, and possibly as high as eighteen million, when the Europeans arrived. Many tribes made it their custom to be welcoming, but the Europeans kept coming, needing more of everything the new continent had to offer. Through the Colonial era, the Revolution and the Indian wars that followed, Northern Indians steadily gave way to the immigrants, migrating to Canada and the West, around and beyond the Great Lakes. But the Cherokee and other tribes in Virginia and the Carolinas, tucked away among hills and hollows, gave up their land more slowly, as did Creek, Choctaw, and Chickasaw across the Deep South. The Seminole and others found ways to thrive in Florida, where swamps and hard-to-farm sandy soil gave them some protection from white migration.

Facing an ever-growing stream of people who had iron, guns, and wheels, and who weren't going to go away, hundreds of thousands of Native Americans reduced their migrations and moved steadily into smaller parcels of land. Tribes that had warred against each other and competed for territory for centuries were forced into each other's laps. Many of them, notably the Cherokee, adopted the English language, European clothes, and names like Bird, Adair, Smith, Pettit, McLean, and McHugh. Some simply blended in, took jobs, married white folks, bought land, and owned black slaves. During that time, it was far more common for Indian women to marry Europeans than for the men to marry European women. Unfortunately, the women's family names were lost in their white husbands' family names. The Indian bride might never see her family again, and when the white family spoke of the couple, they'd just say, "Uncle Henry, he married an Indian."

Then in the 1830s, under heartless orders from President Andrew Jackson, thousands of them were rounded up and moved west,

walking on the Trail of Tears to Indian Territory, the future Oklahoma. Many were forced to move in the middle of winter, and some bled, sickened, and died. Still, a few avoided removal by disappearing into the endless valleys and coves of the deep, green mountains. Also, some lived so deep in the hollows that the soldiers never came for them. A few dropped out of the line during the march and disappeared along the trail. From that time on, it was common for Native American parents to teach their children, especially in mixed-race families like Rosie and Allie Davidson's, to never tell their children that they had Native American blood. That's why so many of today's families pass down whispered stories of Indian ancestors, but are unable to find proof of it in their genealogical records.

All of that—the Indian removals, the Indians who blended in, and the Indians who retained their old culture in remote communities—would have a major impact on what future Americans would eat. On the Trail of Tears, some carried seeds—literal ones like peaches and corn, and figurative ones, like their creation stories—so they could replant in the West. Those who stayed in the East freely blended traditional ways with the best of the new customs and technology, generally becoming successful in white European immigrant terms.

So as hard as Old Hickory tried, he couldn't get rid of all the Indians. Subtly and without fanfare, folks of European extraction learned some things about food from their neighbors, often without knowing they were mixed-blood Native Americans. People of European extraction tend to be linear in their thinking, which has led to innovations like the steam engine and the light bulb, but has slowed their ability to adapt in other ways. For example, an early farmer might have cooked his fish on a grill over the fire, leaving it overcooked and dry. But his Native American neighbor might have taken the time to wrap the fish in wet leaves, then in mud, and place it in hot coals, where the fish roasted as the mud dried, leaving the fish moister and tastier. The Native American people and their culture endured and thrived, which was a good thing, because just thirty years after the Trail, they and their corn would be needed to help revive the Civil War-torn South.

Corn was here in North America, waiting when the first Europeans jumped off their big wooden ships. It began as a wild plant, native to Central America, with tiny kernels on tiny cobs, looking just about the way wheat looks today. It took a lot of work to get a spoonful. So over the course of some 10,000 years, the Natives cultivated and coaxed it into growing bigger and juicier, until there were several healthy varieties, generally known as maize. Then they kept experimenting, frying or boiling it, drying it, then reconstituting it or grinding it into meal, and found that it was great in everything.

There's no way to overstate the importance of corn in the mid-1800s. Sometimes there was no game, the potatoes froze, and bugs ate the squash, but corn rarely failed, even in years of the worst weather. A handful of seed corn produced an equal number of stalks, and each stalk held the promise of one or two ears. Corn could be grown in big fields and crowded corners, and was often planted all the way up to the front door. Corn was vital to pioneers moving west, and by 1900 the Midwest and Western states had become known for their massive corn production. It was raised on vast farms in Iowa, Illinois, Minnesota, Kansas, and Nebraska, as a major cash crop meant for distant tables. Yet corn's impact on family and

community life was greater in the South than anywhere else.

Corn can be boiled or roasted. Everybody liked corn on the cob, and it could even be eaten raw if necessary. Unfortunately, as soon as corn is picked, its sugar starts to turn to starch, and corn on the cob loses its flavor quickly and soon spoils. One way to revive it was by making fried corn with half butter and half bacon grease, adding white sugar or honey, and stirring in salt, onions, and peppers. Some people add tomatoes and celery. Some folks like a little less sugar, but the children like it with more.

When there was a big harvest, farming families preserved it by drying it on racks in the sun or in the corn crib, a shed with slat sides, spaced to allow plenty of air circulation. Once dry, it would keep for months, and could be added to any kind of soup or stew. Best of all, dried corn could be ground into cornmeal, the most dependable and versatile food imaginable. Many a prosperous settlement grew up around the first settler to build a mill on a creek bank. Of course, in almost every hollow there was a creek, and anyone who had a little knowledge in the engineering aspects of water-powered mills could build one. The running water turned a wooden wheel, which turned a spindle that cranked a heavy, round mill stone, rotating on top of another flat stone. Dried kernels were poured into a hole in the top stone, where it was ground between the two, and cornmeal trickled out the edges. But folks didn't have to get their corn to a mill. Everybody knew if they had to, they could grind their own corn at home like the Indians used to do it, with a mortar and pestle.

After the Civil War, agriculture boomed in much of the nation, and the Northern states were home to a flourishing canning industry, which made it possible to ship corn and other

Johanna Lesley is pictured in the 20th century using the traditional American Indian mortar and pestle, near Bracketville, TX. (Courtesy of the Library of Congress)

food, anywhere. Railroads delivered canned goods all over the U.S., except in the South, where the railroads had been decimated by war and were slow to recover. And still, even without corn from Northern canning factories, the ease with which corn is planted and cultivated, the fact that it can be raised in big fields or tiny home gardens, plus its versatility in the kitchen and on the table, meant everything to the revival of the South. So in most of the nation it was a side dish, but in the South, it could be almost anything. Folks used cornmeal to make cornbread, and even added corn to cornbread for corny cornbread. They made johnnycake, the cornmeal version of pancakes. They made cornmeal pie crust, squash bread, bean bread, and fruit-nut breads. Also, cornmeal mush, corn dodgers, fritters, hushpuppies, muffins, soup, and breading for fish, okra, tomatoes, and chicken. Corn cakes could be baked or fried, leavened or not. They fed the cornstalks to cattle and hogs, and in small amounts to horses and mules. Perhaps most important of all, corn became grits.

Today, if we were to ask most people to name the most iconic Southern dish, it would be grits, an answer often accompanied by the joke, "What is a grit?" Grits are ground hominy, and hominy is corn that's had the husks of the individual kernels removed in limewater. The only difference between cornmeal and grits is that grits are a coarser grind, and cornmeal is usually made from yellow corn, while grits are usually made from white corn. A bowl of grits is simply ground hominy cooked in water, and it can be enjoyed in all sorts of ways, with butter, sugar, cheese, syrup, hot peppers, salt, black pepper, and almost anything else that adds flavor. But the original, plain grits is nothing more or less than the staple of the ancient southeastern American Indian diet, which came from an even more ancient Central

American Indian diet. When our ancestors lived in houses made of animal skins and tree bark, they were enjoying the same sort of grits that are served in the glory of the fanciest Southern tables today.

North American Indians traditionally raised their basic three crops, known as the three sisters: corn, beans, and squash. In a small patch, they could grow squash, mulching it with dry grass to keep the ripening fruit off the damp ground. They'd fertilize their crops by burying the heads and innards of fish. They'd make trellises, either in square patterns or simple tripods, for the beans to climb. And there would be a stand of corn, the tallest crop, planted at the north end of the patch so it didn't shade the other plants.

Native Americans made a practice of using corn at every stage, when it was ripe, when it was overripe, when it was dry, too dry, on the cob, off the cob, parboiled, and dried. It could be added to an endless list of stews and soups, or used as the basis of many dumplings and in skillet dishes like succotash. After harvesting the heavy ears of corn in late summer, they'd dry some kernels and keep them over the winter in a hollow gourd or leather pouch for planting the next year. Those corn kernels and a handful of beans and squash seeds were all that was needed to supply the family's basic vegetable diet from their own garden. Virtually every Indian of the eastern tribes knew how to keep such a garden, and save seeds that way. Even after their annual routines were disrupted by the removals to Indian Territory, and even when the lives of those left behind were disrupted again by the Civil War, they were able to reach back for those memories and start doing it again, as their people had done for untold generations.

Native Americans often pulled back the corn shucks without removing them, discarded the silks, then replaced the shucks and covered the ears in about two inches of fresh mud. They laid them in a bed of hot coals and turned them with a rake until they were dry-roasted, which took about ten minutes. Or they'd remove the silks, replace the shucks, tie them together with water grass, and quick-roast the ears. They knew that corn could be dried and preserved on the cob by removing the silks, pulling the shucks back into place, and hanging them on racks high above a slow fire to dry. It might take several days, stoking the smoldering fire the whole time, until the corn was completely dry, but it would keep all winter that way. They knew they could also cut the kernels off the cob and dry them for days in the sun. They had to be dried thoroughly or the germ could sprout during storage, which ruined the kernel and led to mold. They kept their dried kernels in baskets, where air circulated to keep them dry.

The dried corn was brought back to life by letting it soak for a couple of days in a clay pot full of water and wood ashes. The mixture of water and ashes is called potash, and the modern word for the process is nixtamalization. A study of the dining history of humans will repeatedly bring up the amusing question of how some edibles came to be edible. At some point in time, somewhere, one brave soul was the first to break into an oyster, which isn't easy, and then eat the slimy blob inside. Somebody tried each of the mushrooms growing wild in the woods, and some of those experiments ended badly. Somebody got sick eating poke greens, and somebody else found out they didn't get sick if they boiled the greens twice. So how on earth did somebody discover that hardwood ashes soaked in water yield lye, and lye loosens the hulls on dried corn kernels?

In more ancient times, cooks used pots made of animal hide. Such pots didn't survive being heated directly over a fire, so people developed the procedure of heating rocks in the fire, then pulling them out with a deer antler, brushing the ashes off with a grass whisk, and placing them into the water-filled hide pot, where they instantly heated the water to the boiling point. In fact, a good, experienced cook could make the water boil, or could keep it slowly simmering for hours, by carefully controlling the temperature of the rocks. So maybe in the process of moving hot rocks from the blazing fire to a bowl of corn and water, a careless cook failed to brush off the ashes, and gradually ended up with a lot of ashes in the corn. The corn was too precious to throw out, and more important, the accident was probably viewed as the work of spirits guiding the cook to add ashes to the pot. In any case, the cooks all agreed that they had to see where it led, and it led a revolution in corn preservation and reconstitution. After soaking, the cook could simply wash away the skins, or hulls, that were loosened by the ashes, leaving the kernels tastier, easier to chew, and easier to grind into meal. From that moment of that discovery, corn became versatile enough to be used in an endless number of recipes. And it's no stretch at all to say that many a Southern cook bemoaned the fact that they couldn't make a decent meal with dried corn, until a Native American neighbor showed them how to first peel away the hulls from the kernels.

Traditional American Indian varieties of bread include spoon bread, a cornmeal mush made with lots of eggs. It's baked in a clay pot or metal pan, and eaten with a spoon, because it has with a texture like custard. Sarah Rutledge preserved the recipe in her 1847 book, The Carolina Housewife, calling for beating the egg whites, which makes them naturally incorporate air bubbles as they cook, making the bread lighter than cornbread, even though it has no milk, water, or leavening. Audrey Stanfield Asling learned it from her mother, but she also had a modernized recipe that added flavors and textures, including corn, creamed corn, chopped green peppers, sautéed onions, sour cream, and cheddar cheese.

The European Americans loved their salt, but American Indians could take it or leave it, which is pretty much the way Indians are about a lot of things. Salt occurs naturally, sometimes deep in the earth, and sometimes exposed on the surface in salt "licks," so named because animals like to lick them, which is a natural way of getting the minerals they need. So while the white approach was to mine salt with iron tools and haul it away in wagons and on trains, the Indians weren't inclined to such a high technology, mass quantity approach. They preferred to find mineral springs in which the water had a high salt content. Then they'd make a big social event of catching the water and boiling it down until only the salt was left. Everybody got some salt, and everybody got to spend a day of fun with family and friends. Still, when salt wasn't available, they didn't miss it much, and they'd wait for the next gathering at the salt spring. Though Indian fry bread is popular today, Native Americans once made a big variety of boiled and baked breads without grease, and those were breads that would crumble if salt was added to them. There was a whole different list of breads, like pumpkin bread, containing both fat and salt. Native Americans knew they could crush walnuts, acorns, or chestnuts to make nut meal, and use that in place of cornmeal. They even made meal from sweet potatoes and carrots.

One Cherokee staple was bean bread, made by boiling beans, then adding corn meal right into the bean water, and mixing it into bread dough. Bean dumplings could be made by dropping balls of that same batter into a pot of boiling water or grease, and if the cooks used purple-hull beans they'd get blue dumplings. Some cooks preferred making flat bean bread, called broad swords, which called for wrapping patties of dough in corn shucks and boiling them. Cherokee households kept a supply of dried shucks hanging in the rafters of the house or barn for such recipes. When they were needed, a quick steaming would make them supple enough to wrap the flat bread. The cook tied each piece of bread with a piece of water grass, and dropped it into the boiling pot. And when mother was getting the shucks for cooking, she would also grab a few for the children, who used them to make corn husk dolls.

Becky Asling remembers being very young at a family gathering in Arkansas, when her great aunt brought a fist-sized brown ball from the root cellar to the kitchen. She was getting ready to make kinuchi, a Cherokee delicacy. They started by gathering hundreds of hickory nuts and pounding them to break the shells. Then they separated the nuts by hand or by shaking them through a loosely woven basket,

PORCH TALK

According to legend, hush puppies originated among cooks who were preparing big meals, and would drop balls of corn meal, flour, salt, and water into hot grease. The resulting crusty and tasty balls were a cheap, quick, and easy way to appease begging dogs and children. In other words, to hush the puppies. Whatever their origins, creative Southern cooks added onions, cheese, squash, honey, and all kinds peppers and spices, and they've long been welcome at the dinner table.

The seed for this corn was carried on the Trail of Tears to Indian Territory, where it is still grown and shared among Oklahoma's Muskogee-Creek people. (Courtesy of Dana Tiger)

then pounded them in a mortar and pestle until they could be molded into a three-inch ball, with their own natural oils providing the liquid that bound the ball together. The balls were then stored in a cool place, like Becky's great aunt's root cellar. To make the kinuchi, the ball is dissolved by boiling water for about ten minutes, then strained. Very frugal cooks pick out any stray nut meats left in the strainer and put them back in the liquid for the second boiling. When the kinuchi reaches the consistency of light cream, it's ready to eat. Today, most cooks add some combination of hominy, rice, sugar, or salt, for a delicious soup, and kinuchi is still a traditional Cherokee favorite.

The white, European, linear way of thinking contributed to a delightful New World cuisine. But Indians, with their non-linear thinking, and generations of living off the land, made a vast, and all-but-invisible contribution to the diversity of the North American diet. It's probably safe to say that the white folks were slow to add fried cicadas and yellow jacket soup to their menu. But they were probably happy to have their Native American neighbors introduce them to corn, broad swords, and bird egg soup.

Dew sparkles on the leaves of lettuce and tomato plants crowding a late spring garden.

Chapter 7

Tending the Garden

Tomato gravy started with a nice, big skillet. Then it needed some butter and flour, sugar or honey, salt, and pepper. The tomatoes were smashed with a fork, but not too much, because the gravy is supposed to be lumpy. Some milk was added, and as one old Mississippi recipe said, "The milk will sometimes curdle a little bit. I don't know how to stop it, so I just serve it anyway. It tastes so good, folks seldom notice if the milk is smooth or not." Tomato gravy was good on potatoes, pasta, or corn, but everybody's favorite way to eat it was on biscuits for breakfast or lunch. Especially in the wintertime, it was a good way to bring back a taste of the garden.

Even if the soil was rocky, the weather too dry or too wet, the land too shady or too sunny, everybody raised a garden, and the family's survival generally depended on doing it with hard work, planning, and constant attention. Gardens needed plowing, irrigating, companion planting, cultivating, fertilizing, and weeding. Dry land gardens required crops that grew with little, or inconsistent rain, like corn, peppers, potatoes, sweet potatoes, turnips, and rutabagas. But lowland gardens, or those running alongside creeks, might include tomatoes, squash, pumpkins, watermelons, and beans. To cooperate with the moon's gravitational pull, anything that produced its fruit above the ground was planted during the full moon, and root crops were planted in the dark of the moon. Does that make a difference? Plenty of gardeners still wouldn't dream of doing it differently. And while a lot of factors, like an empty pantry or guests coming for dinner, could influence harvest schedules, most garden crops were harvested by the same rules. The moon's pull influenced how much water was in the tops or the roots of plants, so root crops were picked during the dark of the moon, and above-ground crops were picked during the full moon.

Care had to be taken about the height of everything, so one plant didn't shade another too much. That's why garden rows run north to south, rather than east to west. The taller plants, corn, peppers, and tomatoes, along with beans on trellised vines, go on the north side because the sun travels just about straight overhead in June, but is progressively lower in the sky, closer to the Southern horizon, during the rest of the growing season. Shorter crops were lettuce, greens, and the spreading squash vines. The root crops, potatoes, sweet potatoes, carrots, and turnips, could be tricky to grow in the rocky Southern soil. As they grew longer, pushing their way through the clumps and stones, sometimes striking bedrock, with nowhere to go, they could turn out short and misshapen. So if there was a spot in the garden with better, softer soil, that's where the root crops were planted. On the other hand, none of them required a great deal of space. So the enterprising gardener could always find a spot for some root crops over here, and a few more over there.

Planting scattered small gardens, as opposed to one big garden, reduced the chances for bugs and diseases to ruin all of any single vegetable. That was perfect strategy for the South, where rocks, hills, and washouts cut across the landscape. So as a farmer planted in smaller patches, if one didn't produce too well, or was trampled by the family cow, hopefully another patch would survive. If one patch of ground got too wet or too dry, or had too much sun or not enough, maybe the patch of ground on the other side of the house would do better. If worms ate the tomato vines in one patch, they were likely to leave the vines alone in another patch. If a disease attacked the beans on this side of the house, the beans on the other side might not get infected.

Lettuce has become an icon of the healthy modern American diet, and a favorite in home gardens, with its many colorful varieties. But historically, it wasn't central to the Southern garden, simply because there are generally hardier and more versatile leafy green choices. Lettuce has to be eaten soon after picking. Head lettuce, like iceberg, needs cooler weather, and even the leaf varieties are sensitive to the weather, which means they have a short growing season. If a late cold snap comes along and freezes lettuce, then it wilts. In hot weather, it bolts, meaning the stem grows longer and thinner, the leaves become smaller, and seeds form. The seeds can certainly be saved for the next year's planting, but once it bolts, lettuce doesn't produce big leaves for the table.

Spinach is leafy and green, and has a much longer growing season than lettuce. All things considered, if frugal southern gardeners were looking for ways to feed the family, they'd opt for greens that could be eaten raw or cooked, that were easy to grow in changing weather conditions, and that flourished in long growing seasons, or, like many greens, two seasons, spring and fall. Greens were generally boiled with a little pork grease and salt, but they could also be sautéed quickly in a little hot grease, stirring frequently, and mixed with eggs and onions. Collards became a staple of southern cooking, with leaves that grew to about sixteen inches long, providing a lot of food, and the flavor was delicious alone or mixed with other greens. Greens grow so abundantly, many a family ate greens every day, so to create some variety for themselves, they mixed different blends from day to day. That worked out well, because some, like mustard and turnip greens have a peppery taste that many people like only when it's mixed. If there wasn't enough of one green to make a pot, known as a "mess," then a handful of this green and that would make up the difference and add flavor. For all those reasons, mixed greens became a standard of southern cooking.

One of the most popular southern vegetables was turnips, because turnips provide two foods, the starchy root, and the tangy greens. Beets are similar to turnips, but never became as popular in the South because they grow better in colder climates. The turnip itself is hard, small, and difficult to peel. But for a hungry family, it's not too much work. The peel is tough and bitter, and once it's gone, the meat of the turnip can be sliced and boiled with pork grease and salt. After the turnip slices are almost done, the cook can add the greens to the same pot for a good, filling meal. If there's pork to serve with it, so much the better. Beets could be pickled, but turnips were only pickled in a mixture with beets, garlic, and red or chili peppers.

Europeans cultivated cabbage for centuries, and it was extremely popular among German and Irish immigrants to America. It's part of a family of vegetables that includes broccoli and Brussels sprouts, and doesn't like hot weather. That's why European descendants in the North ate a lot of cabbage, using a host of old, traditional recipes, but it was generally less popular in the South. And yet, cabbage found a place in southern gardens because it was so easy to grow and preserve, and it provided a green vegetable when the weather was too cool for lettuce and green beans. It was another of those crops that offered the advantage of two growing seasons, spring and late fall.

There were plenty of German recipes that called for combining potatoes and apples with cabbage, as well as making cabbage rolls with meat mixtures inside. But in the South, where the availability of ingredients was less predictable, recipes tended to be simpler. They boiled the cabbage in a little grease, with salt if they had it. Native Americans have traditionally dried foods to preserve them, and that may be why dried cabbage became popular in the South. People would simply peel the big outer leaves, then cut the head into sections and dry it all in the sun. Dried cabbage would keep a long time in a cool cellar or spring box. They could just drop it into soups, or bring it back to life by pouring boiling water over it, and then it could be sautéed with grease and salt.

Sauerkraut is one of the German imports that became a Southern favorite, simply because it's fermented cabbage, and fermentation has long been a favored preservation technique in the South. Sauerkraut was easy to make by shredding the cabbage and storing it in crocks with salt, water, and perhaps a little wine. Especially for people living in the days before refrigerators, such vegetables that had been long stored away in a cool cellar, served piping hot by the light of a flickering fire, were a welcome addition to the dull winter diet. And sauerkraut became a folk medicinal legend after a series of American flu epidemics. In southern Missouri, when the James Adair family's kinfolks came for an extended visit during the great flu epidemic of 1919, the whole family came down with the flu, except for Nancy Adair and her granddaughter Elida. When they all talked about it later, wondering why only those two had been spared the misery, they realized that only Nancy and Elida had been enjoying some sauerkraut every day from Nancy's big barrel of kraut in the cellar. And from that time on, everybody in the family was sure, "If you eat kraut, you won't get the flu." It may not have been true, but modern knowledge about probiotics and a healthy immune system has given the idea some credence. Besides, as the Adairs said, "What can it hurt?"

Beans have long been a garden favorite because they come in so many different varieties and can be harvested for a long time. Today, seed packets offer several bush beans that can be grown in small spaces and even in pots. But the vintage varieties were all vining plants that needed trellises or fences where they could spread out and get lots of sun to all the leaves. In fact, bean vines can grow to many feet long, but with trellises they take up very little space on the ground. They can even be used to give a little partial shade to other plants that don't tolerate the direct hot sun very well, like spinach and lettuce. There are kidney beans, butter beans, white beans, and green beans, as well as the many peas, from green peas to black eyes, and field peas, also known as crowder peas. The black-eyed varieties as a group even became known as "Southern peas," because they grow so well for

Nancy Adair and her dog are pictured in front of her corn crib, where the corn was stored to dry. Nearby were the root cellar, smoke house, and a fruit orchard.

summers. Beans and peas are also easy to dry, and once dry, can be kept for years.

Shelling peas and beans is a tedious, time-consuming job, and yet in the South, it can be pure poetry. Traditional wisdom says that peas and beans should be picked in the evening, then put into cold water early in the morning, and shelled a little while before noon. They had to be picked when they'd had plenty of water, and when the individual peas or beans could be seen poking their sides out in rhythmic ripples along the pod. But green beans had to be picked before they were too fat and the pods had begun to toughen. Even busy children stopped their play to sit on the porch and help grandma with the shelling. She'd have a basket of long, green pods, and she'd show the little ones how to pop the end from a green bean, peeling it back to remove the string. She taught them how to push a thumbnail into a pea pod, and use the back of the nail to scoot the peas out into a bowl. As the colorful peas or beans filled the bowl, the long afternoon dissolved into sweet conversation and laughter.

Beans are generally boiled in water with a little pork grease and salt. In fact, the Southern way to cook green beans is to boil away nearly all the water so that they end up simmering in mostly grease, with the lid on the pot for a long time, until they're soft. Such overcooked, greasy beans, are part of a preference among Southern cooks to overcook their vegetables. We now know that it's a good way to cook away a lot of the nutrients, but knowing that doesn't make soft, overcooked vegetables taste any less good. There's actually a historical reason Southerners developed a preference for soft, rather than crispy vegetables, and it's the product of the evolving, long-simmering Southern mixed pot. Almost anything simmering on the Southern stove

of the late 1800s was fair game for something to be added to it. Beans might certainly have onions, red pepper, green peppers, bacon, ham, tomatoes, and potatoes added to them. Greens might get any and all of the same. Even carrots, radishes, turnips, and corn might end up in the same pot. And the longer it all cooked, the more the flavors blended. Succotash, a New England Native American dish that became very popular in the South, is made by boiling beans, then sautéing them with corn and plenty of butter or grease.

Small squash could be grown like beans, on trellises and fences, but squash vines are usually allowed to crawl across the ground because the fruit is so heavy. That's the only way to grow the biggest ones, like pumpkin. When the ground is damp, the gardener has to pile a little bed of straw or dried grass under each fruit, so it won't rot where it sits on the earth. There are endless varieties of green and yellow squashes, as well as gourds. Gourds have hard shells, so they could be useful as storage containers, and could even be made into dishes. But the flesh of most of them is edible, and is cooked the same way as other squashes, which means with a little bacon grease.

Nobody can watch a Southern cook for very long without realizing that pork grease and vegetables were made for each other. In the South, in the second half of the nineteenth century, butter was precious, and beef was a relative rarity. Besides, beef fat had to be rendered for cooking. But pork fat, which was abundant and easy to use, emerged as one of two prime ingredients that characterized the reborn Southern cuisine. The other is the pepper.

In the post-Civil War South, spices tended to be hard to find and hard to afford. Sometimes the cook had them, and sometimes not.

A farmer plows his corn field, while two other men follow, planting and covering the seeds. Rows of early spring vegetables can be seen in the background. (Courtesy of the Library of Congress)

Even salt was not a given. And black pepper, which almost everyone expects to find on the American table today, was an import that not everyone in the old rural South could buy. But hot red peppers were easy to grow, dry, and crush or grind, and that's how red pepper became a favorite Southern spice. In fact, the garden out back could yield a steady supply of green, yellow, orange, and red peppers that could be picked at various stages of ripeness to provide a variety of flavors, some getting hotter as they got riper. They could be stored in the cellar or spring house for a few days, but almost all peppers were easy to string on cords and hang in the rafters to dry, where they'd be ready to use all through the winter. So it's no wonder that Southerners developed a taste for spicy foods; they might not always have salt and black pepper, or oregano or rosemary, but by golly, there were always hot peppers.

As long as there've been people in Central and South America, they've cultivated peppers.

There are too many varieties of peppers to count, and not only were they cross-pollinated to produce new strains, but the soil and weather conditions in which they were grown affected their taste, color, and "heat." Why did hot peppers become so popular close to the equator, in the warmest parts of the New World? It's simple science that spicy foods make people sweat, and sweat keeps us cool in hot weather. As our perspiration evaporates from our bodies, it leaves us feeling cooler. Hot weather is a way of life in the American tropics, as well as the American South, so when people eat spicy hot foods, it makes them perspire more, and that feels good.

Although hot peppers were cultivated in Central and South America, they didn't exactly take over the taste buds of the Western Hemisphere. That's partly because Portuguese and Spanish food are not particularly hot, and the Portuguese influenced Brazilian taste, just as Spanish food influenced Central and South American tastes. All of that led to a preference for foods that are only mildly spicy. But when peppers crossed the Rio Grande to the American South, there was little of that Spanish or Portuguese influence to tame them. In typical free-wheeling, beef-loving Texas style, Texans developed preferences for hotter dishes, including jalapenos, habaneros, three-alarm chili, hot sauces, and the popular Tex-Mex cuisine. Yet, the southeastern part of the state, with its seafood, bayous, and cypress stands, has maintained a Louisiana flavor.

So where did people in the rural South get their garden seeds? Not from a store. Stores were far away and seeds were expensive. Instead, they gathered, dried, and shared seeds each year to plant the next year. After a little trading with neighbors, it was rare that a family needed to buy new seeds at all, unless they had acquired more land or were starting a new crop. Why would somebody not save their seed? It just made sense, in a biological way, as well as a philosophical and spiritual way. Every spring the world was refreshed, baby bunnies were born, and last year's seeds started sprouting.

Almost every Southern home also had fruit trees, and many had an orchard with some combination of apples, peaches, pears, cherries, and crabapples. Since fruit trees wear out, people took good care of the new seedlings that came up from fruit that fell to the ground. It was possible to have a rotation, keeping the seedlings, so that the orchard had a mix of new trees, two-year-olds that might bear their first crop, and producing trees from three to eight years old. Cooks were always using their fruit to create different toppings for their cornbread. They made apple butter,

PORCH TALK

In the Boston Mountains of Arkansas, Elaine Stanfield laughs when she tells about her grandmother's applesauce simmering on the stove. It had to cook slowly, for a long time, and couldn't be allowed to boil. The whole time it sat there on the wood stove, cooking just below the point of bubbling, the apples were releasing gases that couldn't get through the thick mixture to the top, and so they built up along the bottom of the pot. The cook had to constantly stir it to keep releasing those gas bubbles. Elaine recalls that if her grandmother got to visiting with some of the cousins and forgot to stir it, that gas would build up and build up and build up until finally, *pop!* It exploded straight up, right through the applesauce, all over the ceiling. And when it happened, the cousins would all just laugh, clean it up, lick their fingers, and start a fresh batch of applesauce.

pear butter, and pumpkin butter. Sometimes they simply boiled a little fruit of various kinds with sugar to make a rich, tasty syrup.

Nothing went to waste in the garden. Gardeners even threw their dirty dishwater on the garden, because the soapy water clung to the leaves and discouraged most of the worst bugs. Any bits of food in the dishwater just fell to the ground and became fertilizer. Weeds had to be cut out of the ground with a hoe, which is one of the oldest human tools. The gardener would walk down each row, chopping and scraping as close to the plant as he dared, although special care had to be taken hoeing around corn, because its roots grew just under the soil. A hoe blade could easily cut one or two, severely cutting off some of the stalk's crucial ability to drink in water and nutrients. In the scorching Alabama sun, every root mattered. The idea of hoeing was to get the young weeds before they grew big and tough. The cuttings could be left on the ground to rot

A visit to the garden can yield a different bounty almost every day during the growing season, like this morning harvest of fresh green beans, mixed greens, and sweet peppers.

into fertilizer. Hoeing didn't get all the roots of all the weeds, but it kept them from taking over, going to seed, and making more weeds.

Mulching is an ancient practice that holds in moisture and nutrients, and it can be done with leaves, pine straw, pine cones, newspaper, or wood chips. Rocks were particularly good around fruit trees, because the dew would condense on the cool stones and drip into the soil. Everything needed fertilizing, and kitchen scraps, even bits of flesh, like fish heads and entrails, could be worked into the soil to feed the vegetables. Unfortunately, that was often a trade-off, because the hogs would have been happy to eat the same stuff that was fed to the garden. One of the best things a farmer could do for his garden was to plow under the garden waste in the fall, so it decayed during the winter and fed the next spring's seedlings.

The family garden was always an exercise in optimism, fueled by an impressive level of creativity. After all, if the family had an abundance of okra, they learned lots of ways to serve okra. Homemade mayonnaise was a staple, lending itself to variations of the basic ingredients, and the cool, tangy taste made it a hit in the South, where it could be used to top almost anything, from cooked vegetables to roast duck, or to make potato salad, chicken salad, and ham salad. There was another similar dressing that was the crowning glory in Confederate slaw, which was a blend of cabbage, "sliced thin as paper," onions, and sweet peppers. That dressing was made with beaten eggs, mustard, sugar, vinegar, milk, and butter. It was heated to blend the flavors, then some cooks liked to pour it over the cabbage mixture while it was hot, which wilted the cabbage a bit and drove the flavors into the crisp ingredients. Others liked to let the dressing cool before stirring it into the slaw, leaving the cabbage crisp. Either way, Confederate slaw was the precursor of what's commonly known as cole slaw, which became popular because it's a cooling counterpoint to spicy Southern meals.

A mother a daughter gather ripe blackberries, dreaming of pies, cobblers, and jam on warm bread. (Courtesy of Library of Congress)

Chapter 8

Nature Provides

The natural abundance of the fields, waterways, and hills, and the lush bounty of the family garden, were two sides of the same coin. Some folks knew every growing thing in the woods, which ones were edible and which were not, and some folks were so good at gardening, they could poke a stick into the ground and it would sprout. Together, with memories and shared knowledge, and in spite of shortages and poverty, they learned to keep fresh food on the table all year long.

Americans have always feasted on what nature provides. People in New Hampshire gather a dozen varieties of wild mushrooms. In Maine, it's blueberries, and in Massachusetts it's cranberries. But the fact is, the father South one travels, the more species one encounters, with some of the most biodiverse regions on earth in North Carolina and along the James River of Virginia. Compare the growing season up north, where it may be five months long, to the Gulf Coast, where it can be ten to twelve months. And that's why gardens, as well as wild plants that are free for the taking, mean more in the South than anywhere else in America.

In the beginning of human life on Earth, people, just like other animals, gathered their food from what was available. They fed themselves with an understanding of the availability of various wild foods at various times of the year, and some of them migrated great distances to find the same perennial foods each year. Then as people spread throughout the globe, they kept trying different foods, their diets changed, and gathering continued to be a pretty good way to eat. Generally, in those days of low technology, gathering could take less time and work, and have generally more predictable results, than either farming or hunting. After all, farmers had to wait for the right time of year, then plant, cultivate, and wait for crops to ripen, and a good crop still depended on the weather, pests, and diseases. Even the most skilled hunters had to rely on their prey to show up, then fall into the trap or wait to be shot or clubbed or stabbed. Then, the bigger the animal, the more work was involved in cleaning, butchering, and preserving the meat. The entire process of eating meat was very inefficient, because hunting, cleaning, cooking, chewing, and digesting meat burned a lot of calories. In contrast to all that luck, skill, and work, gathering wild foods required only a simple walk in the woods or along the lake, picking the same edibles that were picked in those places before, snacking along the way, and taking it home to eat, cook, or preserve.

Gathering was once natural, organic, and common. And like other skills, there were experts in every family, an elder who could walk along, pointing to every leaf, flower, mushroom, bush, fruit, and tree, and say its name, whether it was edible or was good for medicine, whether it tasted good, how to make it taste better, and how to preserve it. How did they gain such an encyclopedic wealth of information, even in the days before books and schools? They learned it by walks with their elders, hearing the same information, and doing the gathering, preserving, and preparing, over and over. They learned it when their headache was cured by chewing on a willow bark, or their upset stomach was calmed with mint tea. And those facts were unforgettable when a day of gathering wild berries ended with a steaming slice of pie.

Today's carefully cultivated grape vines need annual pruning and shaping to produce a good crop, but grapes have always grown wild in the woods, as well as on the family farm fence. Before modern hybrids, early varieties produced smaller, though abundant fruit for years, even in wild and abandoned places, without any help from people. Perhaps the most-loved variety was the muscadine, which bears its fruit in late fall. Of course, grapes don't keep long, so they have to be used or preserved quickly. Fortunately, they dry well in the sun, making sweet, chewy raisins that keep for months. As a special winter treat, Lizzie Tingley baked them into raisin pie, then poured on sweet, rich cream.

Southerners gathered swamp potatoes, an old Native American favorite that can be found flowering in late summer, throughout

People knew what to gather for the table, and they taught their children. With a simple walk in the woods they could find all kinds of good things to eat.

North America, with names like arrowhead, duck potato, and the descriptive water nut, a name that comes from their nutty flavor when roasted. Gatherers harvested these aquatic plants by walking through the water and coaxing their tasty tubers out with bare toes, and letting them float to the top. They could be boiled or roasted. Then in autumn, facing the cold months ahead, people sliced them into medallions and strung them on cords to dry, or pounded them into meal, stored the meal in crocks or jars, and used it like any other meal in breads and cakes. Any food like swamp potatoes that keeps well, even into the depths of winter, was a natural favorite.

Mushrooms abound in the damp, Southern woods. Though many varieties are fatally poisonous, that wasn't a concern to people who learned from childhood to identify and gather morels, chanterelles, and other familiar varieties. Hickory chickens, which some folks call dry land fish because of their slight oyster flavor, are morels that appear in the spring after a good rain, and some local folks were as secretive about where they found their mushrooms as they were about their private fishing hole. Arthur Clinton Casey was kin to almost everyone around Cecil, Arkansas, so the relatives would let him know when the hickory chickens popped up in an area they called "the basin," and then he and his sons would go pick them. His wife Mildred sliced the mushrooms lengthwise and soaked them in salt water, rinsed them, dipped them in an egg wash, rolled them in flour with black pepper, and fried them in bacon grease or Crisco.

Some of the handiest edibles can be found without a lot of training or experience. Most grasses taste somewhat like lettuce, although some of them have a pronounced flavor similar to evergreen or nuts. Clovers, with their familiar three—or four—leaf clusters, can be eaten raw, but taste better boiled. In fact, people have known for a long time that greens provide healthful roughage when eaten raw, but release more nutrition when they're cooked.

Prickly Pear is a cactus associated with the southwest, but was spread by Native Americans throughout the Gulf Coast, where it did well in sandy soils. It's packed with water, and tastes a little like

PORCH TALK

The American chestnut was one of the most common and most impressive trees on the continent when the Europeans came. It grew from coast to coast, with thick trunks one hundred feet tall. The nuts were incredibly difficult to work with, but there were so many of them, foraging people like the American Indians just couldn't pass them up. The meats were packed inside a tough, round hull covered in hard spines that were too sharp to pick up without protecting the fingers. People used a piece of bark to scoop them into gourds or baskets, and carried them home, where they were soaked to soften them. Even then, it took a rock or a stout knife, and strong hands with leather gloves, to open the spiny shell. Oh, but they were worth the effort, because inside were several meats that together were about the size of a pecan. They were too hard to eat, so they were boiled or roasted, or were pounded into meal. So on snowy winter evenings when we hear that old song that says, "Chestnuts roasting on an open fire," it means somebody did a lot of work to enjoy roasting those nuts.

In the early 20th century, chestnut blight came to America on a ship and almost completely wiped out the American chestnut. Today there are other smaller species, and they bear the same needle-shelled nuts, but only a few isolated and hearty survivors of the huge original species remain.

Mushrooms like these, known as oyster mushrooms, thrive in the damp Southern woods. (Courtesy of Tom Barham)

made canteens from the pads. Later, settlers found that it made good jam.

Wood sorrel, also known as sour grass, has clover-like leaves and flowers that come in a variety of colors, and it's a source for both food and medicine. Native Americans chewed it to quench their thirst and to cure mouth sores and stomach aches. The starchy leaves are high in vitamin C, and when they're boiled, they taste like potatoes. Vitamin-packed watercress, which can be found dancing in the sparkling waters along the edges of streams, has a distinct, peppery flavor, so it's not generally cooked with other greens. But like spinach, it can be eaten cooked or raw, in salads, potato dishes, egg dishes, and soups.

Dandelions are good in a fresh salad, or cooked, and like many flowers, the dandelion's blooms are delicious. Wild cabbage is prolific, and grows well into the cold months of the year. It can be eaten raw, or cooked like any other cabbage. Wild onions add flavor to any cooked food, and Native Americans favored them as an addition to eggs. The ramp is a cousin of the wild onion with wide leaves, and like an onion, can be chopped for cooking or eating raw. The crisp, broad leaves of ramps were also used to make wraps, with cooked meat and vegetable mixtures inside. Plantain is a wild-growing plant that was used for food and teas by ancient humans. It not only has tasty young leaves, but is also used as medicine. It's high in several vitamins, and is an especially powerful source of vitamin C.

Chicory is a bushy plant that grows in the South and sports small multicolored flowers. The young leaves are good raw or boiled. The roots are bitter, but they become tasty after parboiling, and then they can be added to soups and stews. But maybe the most popular use of chicory root was as a bitter, warm beverage. The roots were roasted until completely dry, then pulverized with a mortar and pestle, or ground in a coffee grinder, and boiled just like coffee. At the time of the Civil War, coffee had grown to be more popular than tea, and when the great armies ran out, the most popular substitute was chicory root. Even today, the taste lingers on the American palate, thanks in part to New Orleans roasters like Community Coffee, as some people enjoy their coffee with some chicory added.

Then there are the berries, like wild blueberries, which are smaller than today's hybrid blueberries, but grow in clusters, so a little time spent picking can produce quite a yield. Huckleberries are related to blueberries, a little tarter, and even smaller, but are also more prolific in the wild. Both like cooler climates, and thrive in the mountains of Virginia. Blackberries thrive in the Southern summer, ripening about the middle of June. Pickers have to endure their thorny vines to pick them, and many a berry hunter has been known to encounter a black snake sun-bathing in their tangles. Granny Myrtle Simpson took the children to pick them along Cow Creek in Texas, and even made each young one a special berry-picking apron with a matching bonnet. She sewed color-coordinated, neatly-hemmed ties to the bottom hem of the apron, and taught the children to tie them to each other's wrists with a bow, creating a "basket." Then as they picked, they drop the berries in there, and carried them back to the house. Their hands were stained red for days from the berry juice, but they thought it was funny, and Granny Simpson's cobblers were delicious.

Poke greens' mature leaves are naturally poisonous, but the young leaves aren't, so it was really important to know when the leaves were old enough that they wouldn't send a person into fits of vomiting and excruciating cramps. The roots are even more poisonous.

In late summer, the plant grows bunches of purple berries on red stems, and they're only mildly toxic to grown-ups, and a little more so to children. But eating the seeds inside the berries can be fatal to kids. So while the berries were never popular to eat, they were at one time considered a treatment for rheumatism, and were boiled into a tea. It was said to work wonders, as long as it was made and administered correctly. Again, it's easy to see why it fell from popularity if the doctor had to walk such a fine line between giving the patient medicine or poison. In spite of all that, this toxic plant is abundant in the wild and can be easily cultivated, so it rose to such a place of prominence in the South that some towns still have poke festivals.

Sara Jane Hunsaker's grandchildren in Arkansas inherited her Choctaw bloodline, and her poke recipe, which was handed down from her great-grandmother. To remove the toxins, the leaves have to be boiled thirty minutes, and that first water thrown out, then boiled again for fifteen minutes. Then they're chopped up, and cooked in a skillet like other greens, with bacon grease, salt, and possibly sugar or molasses and red pepper. Poke has a stronger taste than most greens, which some people like. Of course, the strong taste is also the reason most people will only eat it if it's mixed with other greens. A lot of people, even knowledgeable writers, refer to poke salad, which is a misunderstanding of the traditional name poke sallet. Sallet is a very old European word for cooked greens.

Nuts were available in endless varieties, so ancient people made nutting stones, with depressions to hold nuts while hitting them with another rock.. Hickory nuts and acorns don't taste very good, but since ancient times, people ground them into meal for baking. Pine nuts are tiny, but they're so packed with protein and other nutrients that they're well worth harvesting. They're only available for a short time each year, when pine cones mature. The cones dry, and as each scale, an individual piece of the hard cone, curls outward, it releases the seed hidden below it. They're too small to find on the ground, so once they fall, they're gone. But if the cones are harvested at the right time, are allowed to finish drying, and then are shaken against a bucket, the little nuts fall out and provide a great snack or addition to salads and recipes.

Little is known about the origins of cultivating pecans, but they were a Native American favorite before the Europeans arrived. In fact, the name pecan is derived from an Algonquin word for nuts that have to be cracked with a stone. Indians enjoyed them with sweeteners, and it was a short step from dipping pecans in honey to the classic pecan pie. Pecans are easier than some nuts to crack, and are relatively easy to shake from the tree, or to knock off with a stick.

Cattails, which grow along the edges of freshwater wetlands, were a staple for Native Americans because they were prolific, easy to harvest, and every part of the plant was edible. The roots and white bottom of the stem, the best-tasting parts, could be eaten raw, or could be boiled, along with the leaves. When the female flower turns brown and dries, it's a cluster of seeds with silky "parachutes." But while it's developing, it can be roasted in the oven or over an open fire, and eaten like corn on the cob. It even tastes a little like corn. Water lilies, another favorite Native American food, reach under water to root in lake bottoms. Native Americans knew that when those roots were boiled, the water could cure sore throat or stomach ailments, including diarrhea. But the roots, as well as the flowers and seeds, could also be eaten raw or dried for cooking later.

American Indians used nutting stones. A nut was laid into the hollow of the stone and struck with another rock to crack it.
(Courtesy of Larry Linhorst)

Along the Gulf and Atlantic coasts, early people gathered kelp and other seaweeds. Some could be eaten raw, and when other salt wasn't available, it could be used to add salt to any dish. It was a healthy, easy-to-harvest food that could be fried or used in soups. It was hung on racks and dried, and could be cooked later, or eaten as a salty snack. But seaweed is an example of a food that never became widely popular because it's available in such limited places, is hard to transport, and is impossible to cultivate on the family farm.

When we think about people of previous generations working long and hard to gather tiny amounts of food, hoping to finally get enough to feed a big, hungry family, it's easy to lose sight of the fact that just like us, they were also on a quest for food that tasted good. And since the beginning of time, people have enjoyed natural teas. Dried leaves and fruits for tea will keep a long time without losing their flavor, and if a family didn't have fine teas from China, they could make their own from wild ginseng, mint, sassafras, plantain, dandelion, and sage. Sassafras is an old favorite that grows in most Southern forests. The beautiful, three-lobed leaves of this tiny tree are easy to identify, and they also have a distinctive smell like root beer. It smells like root beer because sassafras is the main ingredient in root beer, which started as a simple tea made from boiling the roots, then adding a little sweetener. Ginseng root, which grows throughout the eastern U.S., almost to the Gulf, has a bitter taste similar to licorice, and is an ancient medicine to improve circulation and energy. Teas can also be made from most of the edible plants, like dandelion. Pine tree needles, juniper bows, and wintergreen, can also be steeped to make delicious teas, served hot or cold, with or without sweeteners.

Such simple, ageless teas are a soothing reminder that in grocery stores today we still choose from basically the same foods that fed our ancient ancestors. In fact, over 4,000 years ago people were eating most of the popular cultivated food crops of today, including apples, peaches, pears, beans, almonds, onions, watermelons, cabbages, cucumbers, olives, and onions. Most of the fruits we eat, are varieties of fruits that once grew in great wild orchards. The hybrids we generally find in grocery stores today are far removed from the original wild varieties, and the fruits may have some advantages, like ripening slower after picking, but the trees are generally less adaptable and shorter-lived than heirloom varieties. The Newtown Pippin apple, for example, was brought from England to American in the 1600s, and still grows very well throughout the South, from

PORCH TALK

Today, people eat a lot of imported foods, particularly seasonings, which at one time were gathered in the wild. Wild garlic, which is also known as wild onion, grows in several varieties throughout the southeast. Though its bulb is small, like a little green onion, it has a tangy, garlicky flavor. Americans used Canadian wild ginger as a seasoning and a medicinal herb long before ginger was imported and regarded as the essential element in Asian dishes. Wild ginger grows well as far south as Northern Georgia and Alabama, thriving in rich, moist woodland soil. People who grow it mulch it heavily to feed and protect it from drought.

As one elder remarked when a grandchild asked about picking wild garlic, "Sometimes we go in search of a gold coin when there's a treasure chest right here at home."

the Piedmont Mountains through Virginia, North Carolina, and Georgia. Similarly, pears in general do very well in parts of the country that have cooler weather, but some varieties also adapted to the South.

In North America, indigenous people were eating kidney beans, sweet potatoes, peanuts, squash, pumpkin, and tomatoes before the Europeans arrived. And all of those had been cultivated and improved to produce more and better food, after first being gathered in their natural varieties in the wild. Even today, a walk around an abandoned farm might reveal perennial crops, coming up year after year, and slowly reverting to their ancient size and shape. There, on an old fence, might be a hearty vine bearing small beans. In another spot could be a three-inch long squash that, with a little care and time, would produce six-inch squash again. On the hill stands an overgrown apple tree that just needs some pruning to start producing buckets of juicy red apples again, and all around it are apple tree seedlings whispering, "Transplant me to a sunny spot, and I'll give you many more years of sweet apple pies and memories."

In Granville Co., North Carolina, a woman feeds a bucket of table scraps to the family's hogs. (Courtesy of Library of Congress.)

Chapter 9

Meat is Meat

In 1856, the Colt family settled in Kansas near the Neosho River, where pioneer wife and mother Mariam Davis Colt wrote in her diary, "On the banks of the Neosho grow plum trees and gooseberry bushes; along the gulches, ravines, and creeks, grow black raspberries and running blackberries." Mariam also said she was happy for the Stewarts, living a couple of miles away, "where many berry bushes have taken root in the vegetable mould (sic) in their crevices . . .and grape vines clamber over rock, shrub, and tree." There was, "A quiet little lake, sleeping in among the tall grass, whose waters abound in fish and clams," where they shared a claim of 720 acres and "several fresh, cool springs" with about twenty-five other families.

The Colts were members of the Vegetarian Kansas Emigration Company, a spinoff of the American Vegetarian Society in New York. Folks of that era didn't have refrigerators, freezers, all-night grocery stores, or pizza delivery, so they couldn't always be too picky about what they ate. They often had to eat what was available, which meant eating meat. It's hard to imagine being a vegetarian in that setting. Plant-eaters found it difficult to find enough of the right kinds of foods, and especially hard to get good vegetable protein. Just as important, in contrast with today, when being a vegetarian is regarded as a trait of the educated and resourceful, they were regarded as poor and somewhat backward followers of the ancient ways of gathering. After all, Americans of the Colts' era tended to flaunt their ability to buy whatever they wanted, especially meat, and that attitude is partly what inspired some people to rebel by adopting vegetarianism.

By the mid-1800s the no-meat movement was dying out. Some of the enterprising leaders of the Vegetarian Society, which, after all, was a for-profit business, saw a chance to revive it with a profitable colony out west. Ah, the prairie life, thriving on nature's veggie bounty. Or so they thought. But if going meatless was hard in New York, it was impossible on the plains. The Vegetarian Society sent about one hundred New Yorkers to establish a Kansas colony on land about forty miles west of the Missouri line. The new settlers thought it was the perfect place to raise fruits and vegetables. But theirs turned out to be not only the biggest, but also the most tragic such experiment in the West.

The New York organizers, who were supposed to provide all the tools their colonists would need, thought one plow would be enough for the whole settlement. It wasn't. Certainly, the planners' biggest mistake was scheduling their disciples to arrive out there in the heart of winter, when plants are dead or dormant, so they had nothing to eat except the meager supplies they brought with them. And there would be nothing more until they planted the seeds they brought with them, and waited to harvest their crops, which was at least three months away, starting in the summer. Even worse, it turned out to be the year of a bad drought, and all those "fresh, cool springs" went dry. All of them. Mariam Colt had brought fruit trees with her in little wooden buckets, so she planted them, expecting them to bear fruit in their second year. But the drought killed them that first summer. Just when the gardens started to produce, offering a ray of hope, they dried up in the scorching Kansas sun. Mariam wrote that in their struggling vegetarian settlement every meal was pretty much the same—cornbread and the dried apples they brought from New York. Then finally in the fall, as a few late vegetables were finally maturing in the settlers' pitiful gardens, the neighboring Osage Indians, who were also starving, came in the night to take pumpkins and melons. Suddenly the vegetarians became aware of another problem with their settlement: it was in a "no-man's-land" between white settlers and Osages, where nobody was supposed to settle.

Before the end of their first year, the vegetarian Colt family had taken to eating eggs they bought in town. Then they bought chickens to produce more eggs, but ended up eating the chickens, and there went the vegetarian ideal. Then, with their bodies depleted by the hard work of building houses and fences and establishing farms while consuming almost no protein for months, most of the men in the community died, including Miriam's husband and son. About a year after their arrival in Kansas, the tragic colony dissolved.

By eliminating livestock and the West's buffet of game animals from their diet, those vegetarian settlers were betting their lives on an unpredictable mix of wild edibles, crops, weather, and pests. Even for meat eaters like the Osage, it was touch and go out there on the plains. That's why, even though there have always been vegetarians, it's a way of life that hasn't been widely practiced in the South, where eating meat has always been part of healthy survival. Southerners had no reason to go hungry when there was wild game in the woods and fish in the waters all around them. And slaughtering a steer or hog was often a major social event because it would provide rich meat for a lot of people for a long time. It's no wonder that when Dosia Harris was interviewed about her life when she was a Georgia slave, one of the things she talked most excitedly about was eating meat. With a big smile, she described the shared joy of her family as they watched her put beef in a pot to boil, then seasoned it with red pepper flakes and added dumplings.

Spanish colonialists brought hogs to America as early as the 1500s. They generally didn't fence their livestock, and as military posts and settlements moved or were abandoned, some animals wandered and became feral. Horses migrated to the best grass and became the mustangs of today's American west. The cattle grew wild and sometimes mean, also wandering west, and eventually became the foundation of Texas longhorn herds. The wild hogs were the most adaptable of all, because they could scavenge for food almost anywhere, from the Texas hill country to the South Georgia woods and the Florida swamps. They became ill-tempered and dangerous, and the males grew long tusks that could rip a man's leg wide open. But their meat was delicious, and they were a favorite target of hunters. They were so well adapted to the South that no matter how many the hunters killed, their numbers continued to increase.

It naturally followed that over the next

250 years, rural America, especially the South, became home to an odd mix of wild hogs, recaptured and re-domesticated wild hogs, imported European domestic hogs, and cross breeds of wild and domestic hogs. Some farmers kept hogs that weren't far removed from the feral hogs. They were short, slab-sided creatures that still carried the razorback, a strip of long, course hair along their upper spine, a characteristic of their wild ancestors. By the 1880s, domestic breeds were becoming more the norm, especially on the bigger farms. In rural communities, it was quite common for farmers to let their hogs roam free, and it was hard to fence them in anyway, because as they rooted in the ground for food, they pushed down rails and dug out fence posts. Town councils had long debates about whether they needed an ordinance forbidding the hogs to wander the streets. It was a question that was generally easy to resolve, because domesticated pigs, high bred or not, had little interest in running off, with or without a fence.

On the other hand, they were easily spooked. Sometimes the slightest surprise could send them off on a short sprint in any direction. That made them difficult to drive in any number. Another annoyance was that it was their nature to forage as they were being driven. They'd meander, sniffing the ground, instead of watching where they were going, so drovers had to constantly remind them with long sticks to get back in a bunch. A trip to market with anything more than about three or four pigs required a couple of men just to keep them going in the same direction. It couldn't be done from the back of a horse, but of course those characteristics made hogs even more perfect for poor Southern families who may not have had a riding horse anyway.

Out West, on the broad prairie grasslands, ranchers could raise great herds of thousands of cattle that would mill about, more-or-less staying with the herd, without fences. That gave rise to the western ritual of spring roundups and branding. Cattle roamed freely through the winter, and then when the weather warmed, the ranchers would ride over vast prairies, gathering every bovine they could find. They'd check the brands to identify which ones belonged to which ranch, and new calves that had been born through the winter months were matched to their owners by their mother's brand, and were also branded.

Of course, cattle could wander off, and they were prone to stampede because they were spooked by lightning, or a cougar attack, or even a sudden noise on a quiet night. And if that happened, in their panic they might run a long way before tiring out or being stopped by a natural barrier like a hill, gulley, or river. But still, it was not too hard for a man on a horse to see a big herd of cattle across the great, flat grasslands of the West, and go round them up again. For all those reasons, cattle flourished out west, and not so much east of Texas.

East of Texas, in the South's kaleidoscope of steep, wooded hills, mountains, watersheds, and winding roads, the views weren't so vast.

PORCH TALK

For poor folks who were desperate to feed a hungry family, almost any bird would do, and if nothing else, they would turn to crow. Nobody liked the taste of crow, and was only served as a last resort. Just like today, when we find that we're wrong about something, there's no excuse, as a last resort, we have to eat crow.

In fact, some of the woods were so thick with trees and underbrush, two people couldn't see each other standing twenty feet apart. There were some small cattle herds, and many families tried to raise a calf or two every year. But those animals had to be kept behind good, strong fences, because if they got out, they disappeared into the rich, green hills and coves and might never be found. The big problem with fencing cattle and horses, is that they push, chew, and step on fences, clear proof that they believe the adage that the grass is always greener on the other side. Anyone who owns them has to be constantly vigilant about checking their fences and repairing them. It's not a question of whether they'll need repair, but only how often.

Some Southerners kept a few sheep and goats too. They don't destroy fences like bigger animals do, but because they're smaller, they require tighter fences. Goats don't like to be confined, and if goats get out, they can run quickly over the roughest terrain, and can be very hard to round up and bring back home. Until very recently, the varieties of sheep available in America couldn't stay healthy in the heat of the South, and sheep are very susceptible to Southern parasites. An even bigger problem with sheep and goats is that they need a lot of grass. The structure of their mouth allows them to crop grass closer to the ground than cattle and horses, and they need relatively big pastures so the grass can grow back. If they're kept in a small corral, they'll soon kill the grass and end up living on a patch of dirt with nothing to eat.

A farmer in Hidalgo Co., Texas, used wire fencing to make a combination chicken coop, hog house, and mule barn. (Courtesy of Library of Congress)

But in the South, pigs were perfect. Following the Civil War, hogs came to dominate the Southern dinner table and economy, mainly because they didn't need much land, and a lot of pigs could be kept quite happily in small pens with crude fences along rocky hillsides. When they killed the grass and trees, they were happy in the mud. They would eat any kind of vegetable, fruit, or even meat scraps, and if the farmer had nothing to feed them they could find their own food, because they were natural foragers, using their tough snouts to dig up roots and grub worms. In fact, their digging and destruction of roots could be useful in killing seedling trees that the farmer needed to clear for more planting and pasture.

Across the South, late fall to early December was hog butchering time. In the crisp air, surrounded by colorful leaves, ripening pumpkins, and trees full of apples and sweet persimmons, people would walk from farm to farm for the annual hog killing, turning the heavy, dirty work into a neighborhood social occasion. Hogs provided ham, chops, bacon, sausage, salt pork, ribs, loins, chitterlings, chewy pickled tails and feet, organ meats, and tough hides, and the dogs got the dried ears to chew on. As they were slaughtered, fresh pork was packed in cheesecloth bags or old flour sacks. Some meat and trimmings were ground with sage and other spices to make sausage. Most of it was cured and stored to be eaten throughout the coming year.

In the years of increasing abundance leading up to the Civil War, Americans expected meat in the center of the table, and thought of everything else as trimmings. During that same time, there was a trend for city dwelling families, and even those on the bigger producing farms, to buy more and more of their food from stores and from other farmers, partly as a practical matter, and partly as a show of wealth. A rice plantation, for example, might devote as much land and labor as possible to producing their money crop, while buying most of their meat, milk, eggs, and produce. It was the new American way, and just seemed to fit in with the national psyche, asserting the abundance of the newly independent nation.

Then in the South after the Civil War, with the livestock all but wiped out, it was infinitely harder to put meat on the table. If there was any meat in the stores, it was too expensive for most families. Hunters took to the woods and fields, only to find that the wild game was also nearly gone. Not only had the huge, swarming armies harvested most of the game, but around battle sites and everywhere they camped, they had overgrazed and trampled the grass, and felled the trees for fortifications and firewood, leaving everything from bears to deer to squirrels with no decent habitat. Then the Great Drought of 1867 made it even worse. Bigger animals need more feeding range than smaller ones, so they were most affected by the devastation of war and drought. A hunter might find a deer, turkey, or hog in a remote hollow, but they certainly weren't as plentiful as they once were. And fewer trees meant there were fewer squirrels, rabbits, birds, and raccoons. Deforestation and drought meant more soil erosion, which filled waterways with silt, slowing them and reducing the amount of oxygen they carried. As a result, fish were harder to find, and the native brown trout all but disappeared from the South.

And yet, below the surface of a thousand meandering bayous, catfish still lurked, some of them growing to thirty pounds or more. The bigger rivers with their inlets and bayous, were still supporting some bass, perch, and sunfish. And all of those fish could be fried, perhaps the South's favorite way to enjoy fish, and served with ketchup or blends of mayonnaise and relishes, the Southern version of tartar sauce. They could also be baked in the oven or roasted over a fire, and it only takes a little bit of fish to make a lot of fish soup.

Besides, when you're hungry, meat is meat. Folks along the coast could still dig for crabs and clams, and those along the rivers gathered mussels and crawdads. People were proud to eat possum, squirrel, raccoon, groundhog, and snake, all of which could be killed without guns, using traps, snares, stones, and clubs. That was crucially important to some families who couldn't afford guns and ammunition. The biggest snakes were the timber rattlers, found in the rocky outcrops of almost every Southern state. They could grow to six feet long and as thick as a man's fist, so one snake could provide several pounds of meat. Rattlesnakes were best when skinned, then cut into pieces, breaded, and fried. Besides, they were easy to clean, and the skins provided beautiful, decorative leather. It was too thin to be useful as a strap or harness, but it sure made a nice hatband. Freshwater eels are scavengers, and their blood is toxic, but not when cooked. An eel was a little easier to prepare than a snake, because it could be cut into two long filets, then fried, baked, or roasted, so both freshwater and saltwater eels became very popular, and recipes for preparing them abounded.

From ancient times, people found mussels, fish, turtles, and crawdads in fresh water rivers and streams.

Throughout history people have enjoyed songbirds, studied them, written poetry about them, and been amazed at their rainbow of colors and the variety of their songs. But again, meat is meat, and a bird in the hand is delicious, even when the bird's breast is the size of a silver dollar. There was a time when people ate a lot of small birds, especially in the South, with so many of them flitting and singing through the rich forests. People ate pigeon, dove, quail, and little water birds called sora, along with the eggs of all those birds. The breast was taken, and depending on how many birds the cook had, they might fry them, or bake them. If there weren't enough of them for the main course, a couple of pigeon breasts might have been a nice addition to boiled potatoes, a stew, or vegetable soup, sometimes along with other meat. If the hunter brought home a dozen or so small birds, they'd be gutted, skinned, and washed, then put between two towels, and rolled with a rolling pin to flatten the bones. Then they could be fried, boiled, or baked, but they were most often broiled. Like any meat that has no fat, they required a lot of butter, and were often served with a mushroom and wine sauce. Quail were good wrapped in grape leaves and baked. Perhaps the most labor-intensive, not to mention strangest, bird recipe was that for jugged pigeons. The birds were beheaded, skinned, and gutted, then the liver was lightly roasted, mashed, mixed with eggs, bread crumbs, and spices. That mixture was then stuffed into the pigeons and they were sewed shut before being put into a stone crock. The crock was set into a pan of cold water, then boiled for three hours while water was added to keep them covered. Jugged pigeons were served with lots of butter, and maybe gravy too.

If meat is meat, an egg is an egg, especially in a cake. If a farmer had no chicken eggs, almost any egg would do. Wild bird eggs were so small, and the nests so hard to find, that they were hardly worth the work to collect them. But turkey, quail, and water bird eggs were prized. Duck eggs are bigger, and although they have a peculiar taste to them, hungry folks can learn to enjoy lots of peculiar tastes.

To bring home some birds for dinner, folks didn't have to go into the field armed with shotguns. In fact, poor folks might have needed to conserve their bullets, or might not have had ammunition, or might have even sold their guns. Guns were about the last things a desperate family sold, but sometimes things got so bad they had to get some cash out of the last hunting rifle. As a result, some people became expert at killing birds and other small game by setting snares and throwing rocks, just as their ancestors had done for thousands of years. Women seemed to be especially good at using stones as weapons. They were generally more patient than men, and could get closer, then ping the prey with a rock. It would spook the rest of the birds in a group, but sometimes they'd only hop, rather than fly away, so that a stealthy hunter with good aim might be able to get a few more.

At the other end of the violence spectrum was alligators. In the quest for gator meat it was often unclear who was the predator and who was the prey. They'd been hunted for generations in the swamps from Georgia to Louisiana, starting with ancient methods that called for stealth and a couple of men with clubs. Later, a stout lasso and a hatchet would do the job. But a man with a gun could almost be sure to bag a gator safely, as long as he didn't lose a leg to the gator's friends lying in the brush.

Alligator meat was tough, so it was better when cut into small chunks and cooked slowly for a long time. A big gator provided dozens of pounds of meat with virtually no fat, and the tough texture made it perfect to smoke or dry in the sun, which is known as jerky. Gators lived with the fish, and they ate fish, so they tasted a little like fish. Of course, they also ate birds, rodents, and an occasional goat or pig, so they weren't quite as fishy as fish.

The texture of gator meat is somewhat like turtle meat, but a turtle's flavor is milder. If the children didn't grow up eating turtle, it might take some convincing to get them to try it. When J. R. Simpson, who lived on the Texas coast, told the grandchildren he was going to make turtle soup, his young audience revolted. "Ok," he said, "I'll make you fried chicken instead." The hungry children enjoyed their dinner and said it was the best fried chicken they'd ever tasted. Only then did he tell them the fried chicken was fried turtle. According to one former slave, Uncle Robert, of Houma, Louisiana, "If folks didn't know the difference, they'd think turtle was chicken. That's after they're cooked, of course," he'd say. "Most folks can see the difference between a turtle and a chicken before they're cooked.

Turtles were one of the animals that could be hunted with or without guns. Some people hunted them by hand, reaching into the holes along the riverbank. Hunting turtles that way, called noodling, was as old as people. The hunter would keep the back of their hand along the top of the hole and slide it back, then reach down to see if they felt a turtle shell. If so, they tried to grab the back end. The turtle backed into its hole, so it would always be facing out, meaning the hunter could pull it out and grab the front end of the shell with his other hand. He or she just had to be really careful to avoid the jaws. It was a lousy trade to feed the turtle a finger so the family could have a meal.

Another ancient way of catching turtles was the turtle trap, which could be built quickly by men, women, or children. They located a likely turtle habitat, like a swamp, backwater, or pond, and built a circle of rocks big enough to stick above the surface of the water, leaving an opening in one side, curving in, and narrowing into a funnel. Then they baited their trap with almost any kind of rotting meat. In fact, even fresh meat would do, because in the warm, Southern water it would rot soon enough. The stench of the meat would spread through the water and attract the turtle, which navigated and poked around the ring of stones until it swam down into the funnel. Once inside, it found the smelly prize, but after enjoying a meal couldn't find the way out. The hunter just came back later and picked up the turtle.

A kid who was new to turtle hunting, maybe a cousin visiting from town, was sometimes given the job of getting the shell off. After the hunter cut the turtle's throat to kill it, he'd give the turtle to the child with instructions to hang it up by the tail on the barn wall and watch it until the shell fell off. "You have to watch," they'd be told. "If you take your eyes off of it, the shell will never fall off." Of course, a turtle's shell is part of its skin and won't fall off, so after an hour went by, and the poor kid still sat beside the barn with eyes watering from staring at the dead turtle, some soft-hearted soul would come and tell him he was the victim of a joke, and the child would endure the family's giggles. It was harmless rural fun, and the kid was sure to use it on the next unsuspecting cousin who came visiting from town.

Turtles could be caught almost any place there was water. Everybody knew that in the summer, you kill the turtle at night, but in winter, you kill it at daylight. Nobody was quite sure why. That's just the way it was done. You hung it up by a back foot to bleed it out from the neck, and one cookbook said, "After breakfast, scald it and scrape the outer skin (scutes) off the shell." Again, nobody was sure why that job needed to be done after breakfast, but that's the way it was done. The kids often got the job of smashing the shell into pieces, which went right into the soup pot. It was too tough to eat, of course, but the gelatin that boiled off of it added flavor and body. The legs, eggs, and other tender, meaty parts were set aside to fry. The rest went into the soup pot with onions, parsley, thyme, salt, pepper, allspice, and according to some cooks, variations of cayenne, lemons, burnt brown sugar, curry, cloves, and marjoram. Some tied the spices in a cloth bundle so they imparted their flavor, but didn't become part of the soup. One thing they all agreed on was that turtle soup needed about a cup of wine, which not only added flavor, but also tenderized the meat. The soup had to cook very slowly, and about an hour before serving, they thickened it with a flour and butter mixture. It was a lot of work getting turtle soup to the table, but the number of different recipes, both handed down in family tradition and in cookbooks, shows how popular it once was on the farm and in the city.

Turtle shells were handy bowls, and they cost nothing. They're made of keratin, just like fingernails and hooves, and they can be beautiful, with patterns of brown, green, black, and gold when hit by sunlight. Some were so pretty they were hung as decorations on porches and barn walls. If they were rubbed with a little fat every couple of years, they'd shine and last forever. When they were dried in the sun, the outer layer, the scutes, peeled off, so the shell could be used for crafts. Turtle shells have been used for centuries to make necklaces, bracelets, hair decorations, banjo picks, lamp shades, and earrings.

Fortunately, by the third quarter of the 19th century, the wildlife habitat that had been diminished by the Civil War came back, and the wild game of the Southern states was once again abundant. There were plenty of people who knew how to hunt, including men who had hunted for the army or the railroad work crews. And dividing lines between genders were blurred when it came to hunting. Men might have done most of the shooting, but the South has long been known for women who are good with guns and traps. An early shotgun, with its iron and steel barrel could weigh thirty pounds, making it a chore to carry around in the field all morning. Then technological advances after the war included better designs and lighter steel barrels, all of which contributed to the popularity of feeding the family from the land. That continued well past 1900, in spite of the fact that it was an era when people were becoming more urbanized. As Southern cities and towns grew, the South also became rich in public lands where hunting was allowed, as well as private land and hunting club preserves. State and federal governments managed wildlife, including fish hatcheries, and hunting laws, which had been around since colonial days, were refined, with more sensible limits.

PORCH TALK

Wise fishermen say, if you're fishing and catch a carp, don't throw it back. Filet it as you would a bass, then soak the filet in buttermilk. Put it on a cedar plank that's been soaked in water, and season the carp heavily with your favorite spices. Then place the plank on hot coals and cover it with a wet rag. Cook it for fifteen minutes, remove it from the fire, scrape the carp into the fire and eat the plank.

The task of hunting, bleeding, gutting, and butchering a big animal like an elk, deer, bear, wild hog, or turkey, has always been a lot of work. But once it was butchered, it could be smoked, dried, or cured in salt, and it was worth all that work to get ten pounds of turkey meat or almost 200 pounds of elk. Big game was a treasure, and yet the quest for meat wasn't necessarily about bagging a giant deer or a hulking bear that would feed the family for months. It often came down to simply getting something for the next meal. People also hunted ducks, geese, and smaller game like squirrel, rabbit, raccoon, muskrat, and woodchuck. They took the meaty parts as a main course, and rather than cleaning all the meat from the smaller, bonier pieces, those just went into the soup pot. Some people ate possum, but the meat was dark and greasy, and because possums ate anything they could find, including carrion, moles, and snakes, they smelled disgusting while cooking. On the other hand, muskrats and field rats were clean vegetarians that were always welcome in a stew. Some folks thought they were even better dipped in cornmeal, and fried until they were crunchy. But if the hunter wasn't careful removing the muskrat's red musk glands, his family was in for a putrid supper.

Young animals are naturally tender, while the meat of older animals can be tough and stringy. Big game tastes best and becomes more tender if it's aged in a cool place for a week or so before butchering. It can also be tenderized by pounding it with a mallet to break up the meat fibers, or by marinating it in mixtures of oil and acids, like wine or vinegar, and also by slow, patient cooking over a low fire. Wild game has a strong taste, which takes some getting used to for most people today. Our ancestors grew up with that taste, and still, cooks usually took away some of that wildness by soaking or parboiling the meat in salt water. Game animals have very little of the fat that characterizes meat from domestic animals, simply because they eat a completely natural diet and are more active. But the fat they do have is very strong tasting, and must be trimmed away before it's cooked. Then pork grease or lard is added when cooking it, or sometimes cutlets are wrapped in bacon, to keep the meat from drying out. Even with that added grease, it's still very easy to overcook game, leaving it dry, which is one of the reasons Southerners developed such a preference for a broad variety of ketchups, sauces, relishes, and gravies.

Hunting has long been part food-gathering and part ritual, woven into Southern culture and family life. It's a gift from one generation to the next, as much as Christmas mornings and work ethics are gifts. While there are people who question whether it's fair and right to hunt wild animals at all, such conversations are decidedly rare in the South. And it's not only because grandparents' grandparents stocked their larders with wild game. It's that, plus a lot more. Southerners have seen their families nourished by both the animal and vegetable gifts of nature, and have an innate understanding that it is the order of things.

To this day in the South, even those who've never hunted or fished, and don't eat wild game, understand hunting and fishing. There's an unspoken feeling that a non-hunter could be plopped down in the middle of the wilderness with a single-shot .22 rifle or cane pole in hand, and could return home with dinner. Not because it's easy, but because it's in our blood. Hunters and fishermen are famous for their bragging, not only about the size and ferocity of their prey, but also about their own skill and cunning. Their stories reveal that deep inside they know better than

The members of an 1890 hunting club pose after an early-winter hunt with their bounty, including a deer, turkeys, and ducks.

anyone how smart and strong the animals are, and how hard it is to bring one to the table. In the Native American view, even a skilled hunter depends on a deer or turkey or fish, or whatever he's hunting, to give itself up so that the hunter and his people can have something to eat. Every living thing sooner or later gives up its place so that others may live. In hunting and fishing, a Southerner sees the circle of life, the relationship of all living things, and the rebirth that comes with death. It's both good book and cookbook, scripture and recipe.

When the hunter is elbows deep in blood, cleaning the entrails from some creature that was enjoying its breakfast a few minutes before, there's a direct spiritual connection, even if the hunter isn't aware of it in that moment. Give him enough time, a chair on the porch, and a piece of pie after a big meal, and the hunter might be able to talk about what it all means. It's not one part of the experience, but rather the whole of it that resonates, beginning with dreaming of the hunt, scouting for animal signs, like tracks, rubs, hair, and droppings. Then there's following the game trails, locating dens and beds, and planning where and when to do the hunting. For the hunter, it's the early rising on a cold, misty morning, the whispered prayer for a successful hunt, the concentration of quiet stalking, the tightening tension of listening, the pounding heart when the prey is spotted, and the adrenaline rush with the booming gun or the arrow's whistle pierces the pastoral scene. For the fisherman, it's quietly walking the riverbanks, keeping his reflection off the water, watching the currents, and looking below the glistening surface to see which fish are feeding in which spot. Today, some do it on the sandy bank of a farm pond with Great Uncle Bill's cane pole, and some from a radar-equipped speed boat on the lake that was formed by a power plant dam. But either way, at its essence, it still boils down to matching wits with crafty fish the same way our ancestors did. And like our ancestors, we still end a successful hunt or fishing trip with the tedious business of cleaning and butchering. In the end, it always leads to a trusted recipe and the grease sizzling in the skillet. The whole process melds into the familiar picture of the family gathered around a one hundred-year-old table, with life-giving meat served on heirloom plates, while retelling the old stories and lifting up thanks for one more meal and one more day.

Chapter 10

The Whole Hog

When a big group of family and friends got together in the old South, roasting a whole hog was a perfect way to mark the occasion. They chose a fat hog. They chopped its liver and mixed it with bread crumbs, eggs, and lots of butter, and then sewed that mixture into the pig's belly, where its innards used to be. Traditionally, they put it on a spit and roasted it, while basting it with lard. They could also baste it with its own drippings, but lard gave it a nice crispy outside. Whole pigs could also be cooked in a pit in the ground, where a pig-length fire has burned down to hot coals. But it took a tremendous amount of preparation and work tending the fire, then covering it with a thin layer of mud, green branches, or stones, and laying the pig in there so it cooks, but doesn't come in direct contact with the coals. Besides, anyone who's ever tried to dig a posthole in the sunbaked Georgia clay can understand why this method works great in the sands of Hawaii, but was never as popular in the South. And there's a reason for the old familiar image of a roasted hog with an apple in its mouth. A pig that's on a spit needs the apple to hold the mouth open so that as steaming gases expand inside during cooking, they can escape through the mouth. A good picnic could sure be ruined by built-up steam exploding a pig's belly.

The point of the expression "the whole hog" is to eat or otherwise use the entire animal.

Some people today don't even like to look at raw meat, but our ancestors couldn't afford to be so picky. When Papa got up before dawn to come home before noon with a bag of squirrels or a couple of turkeys, Mama and the kids had to do their part. People who caught, hunted, raised, slaughtered, and butchered their own meat were ready and able to prepare and eat all the parts. All the parts. It was a common job for the first two hundred years of American cooks to roast a pig, cut off the head, split the face, remove the chops and ears, then put it all on a big serving platter with dressing and plenty of drippings. And those "whole hog" ways held on in the South long after other parts of the country had grown too sophisticated to eat brains.

Pioneers used the whole animal, never knowing when their next meal might come along. Poor folks did it, trying to make everything go a long way. So did slaves, living on meager rations. In the Native American tradition, it was not only practical, but also spiritual, showing gratitude by letting nothing go to waste.

All across the South, people ate crawfish, also known as crawdads or mudbugs, by boiling them for a few minutes with spices. Or by parboiling them and removing the shells, and then frying the tails until they were crispy. Devoted crawfish fans still suck out the contents of the heads and claws. A lot of people eat frog legs, but there's more to a frog than that, with plenty of meat on a big bullfrog's breast and front legs. Hungry southerners would clean a frog like any other game, skin it, then boil it, and finish with breading and frying it.

Squirrels are about the same. If one is skinned and cleaned, it yields four scrawny legs, some stringy side meat, and that's about it. So hungry folks had ways to use it all. They'd clean out the innards, then singe off all the fur over an open flame. Everything that was left, skin and all, could be roasted or put into the pot with potatoes and carrots for a yummy stew. One popular recipe was creamed squirrel on biscuits. For frying, the squirrel was cleaned and skinned, then quartered, just about like quartering a chicken. Then each piece was dredged in flour with spices, then in egg, then in the flour again, and fried in an inch of hot grease. In the spirit of letting nothing go to waste, most people roasted or fried the heads along with the rest of the animal.

When Mama Ruth Barham's grandchildren were visiting her in Cass, Arkansas, they slept

PORCH TALK

Sweetbread is organ meat, and though the name has been used for various innards, it's actually the throat or pancreas of an animal, usually a calf. Sweetbreads were generally soaked in saltwater, split, buttered, and breaded with salt and pepper, then fried along with the liver. Of course, without the breading they were also added to other dishes, including soups and stews. Nothing could be more poorly named than sweetbread, because it has a distinct taste that most people describe as tasting like what it is: innards. With any luck, that taste disappears in recipes.

in four double beds in the back bedroom, and she'd come in to wake them, banging a spoon on a pot. She always had fried squirrel on the breakfast table, along with country ham, red-eye gravy, fried eggs, fried potatoes, biscuits, and fresh tomatoes. The kids' grandpa, Daddy Miles, always wanted the squirrel heads, swearing their brains were the best part of the meal. "If squirrels didn't have brains, the family might have all been vegetarians!" he opined. Then, cracking the head open with the handle of his butter knife, he announced, "Squirrel brains, they make you smart!"

Squirrel skin was thin enough to eat, but the hides of cows, pigs, bears, deer, and other big animals are notoriously too tough to chew. And yet, when an animal was skinned, the hide was available to the cook, along with everything else, so some folks used it. The Cherokee people even went as far as making meat skin soup. They cut the hide into strips and boiled it, then put it into a pot with a little cornmeal and salt, and boiled it some more. If vegetables were available, those could also be thrown in. With enough cooking, it made a tasty, though chewy, soup.

Meat of any kind was often stretched to feed more people or to make several meals by putting it in a soup or stew. While a good day of fishing would supply enough to fry, even a bad day of fishing might supply enough for fish soup. And even if the fish didn't bite at all, the fisherman didn't need to go home empty-handed. He might bring home a few clams or crabs from the sea shore, or mussels or a turtle from the river, and those would go into the soup.

Dressing and preparing the meat was a job that fell to whomever was available. Nobody could be squeamish about it, because getting meat to the table often meant getting covered in warm blood. From the earliest age, boys and girls knew where their food came from

Southern children learn early the joy of getting up before dawn to stand on the bank of a stream with a pole and a tobacco can full of worms, and returning home with meat for the table

and which parts they were eating. They saw animals breed, have babies, get doctored, get milked, and get killed, cleaned, and butchered. It went right along with raising gardens, tending orchards, and gathering nuts, berries, and roots. These were people who picked fat, squishy green tomato horn worms off their tomato plants. They'd cut open a squash vine to get the worm out before it killed the plant, then cover the vine's surgical wound with fresh dirt. The whole family would line up and walk through the corn field, peeling the shucks back on each ear, picking out any worms, and closing the shucks again. If a mule showed up with a flap of skin hanging loose where it cut itself on a rusty nail, somebody would hold a rope twist on his nose while somebody else sewed him up. They had an intimate, organic relationship with the land and everything that lives on it that can only be learned by being in touch with those things as part of daily life.

Freshly-killed animals like hogs were hung up to bleed out, and it wasn't uncommon to use the blood from big domestic animals. Up north, the Germans had their Blutwurst, or blood sausage, which they made in endless varieties with all kinds of fillers and spices. But the southern version could be made with fewer ingredients. When an animal was butchered, they just put some salt in a bucket and caught the blood. They'd clean the stomach, then pour the blood in, add grease, and add red-hot rocks to cook it until it became blood pudding. Yummy.

In cleaning an animal, great care had to be taken not to puncture the kidneys, bladder, and intestines, because the fluids from any of those would taint the meat. But then, many other organs were saved from the mess, because they made mighty fine eatin'. The hunter field dressed a big animal where he killed it, opening the gut to scoop out the entrails, mainly the intestines, which lightened the carcass enough to get it home. The cleaning couldn't be done up next to the house because first, it would smell terrible the next day, and second, it would draw every kind of scavenger, from flies to bears. But smaller animals, including fish, could be brought home and cleaned close to the house. A well-equipped family had a gut bucket that could be dumped out in the woods. All those innards went into the food chain as they were eaten by everything from bacteria to vultures and coyotes and bears, so that in the big picture, the waste helped feed the critters the family would be eating next.

Among the organs that were saved, each had its own texture, with kidneys being soft, but solid. Kidneys and brains of beef, deer, and hog, were stewed, grilled, broiled, and croqueted. Most folks liked kidney fried in grease with plenty of salt, onions, thyme, garlic, and some red pepper. Hearts are very tough because they're hard-working muscles. They were cleaned like a green pepper, cutting away the tough valves, then slicing, breading, and frying it. They were also roasted or boiled, and sometimes served with tongue on toasted bread. Getting the brains out meant splitting the skull with a hatchet. The brain has the consistency of gelatin, because it's about ten percent fat. Brains required a lot of washing to get rid of the blood and membranes until they were perfectly white. Then they could be added to soups, but they were usually beaten with eggs, and cooked with some combination of lemon, thyme, parsley, and other spices. Brain croquettes were made by rolling a brain-egg mixture into balls, dipping them in milk, then more egg, then bread crumbs, and finally frying them in lard. For a nice presentation, flat, fried brain cakes were served on the baked head meat in the family's best deep dish.

One morning Grandma Ella Armstrong made calf brains and eggs for her granddaughter, Laurel, who was willing to try eating anything, and her brother Howard, a notoriously picky eater. No matter how much Grandma begged and encouraged, Laurel just couldn't even bring herself to taste it. Then she looked over at Howard, the picky one, and he was stuffing the breakfast down as fast as he could go. Years later, Laurel decided to ask her brother about that morning at Grandma's breakfast table. "How did brains and eggs taste?" she asked. Howard answered. "I saw the grief you were going through, not wanting to eat it, and knew it must be awful, so I just dumped ketchup all over it, and it was fine. Tasted like ketchup."

Bread rarely lasted long enough to go stale, but if it did, it was never thrown out. Stale bread, if kept dry, would keep for a long time. Then it would have another life when it was pounded into crumbs for breading. For example, liver of almost any animal was worth breading and frying. Beef, sheep, pig, and turkey testicles were breaded and fried, and known as calf fries, sheep fries, pig fries, and turkey fries, or the simple euphemism mountain oysters, and they became the centerpiece of many community harvest celebrations.

Calves' feet and pigs' feet were treated alike, being boiled until the meat came easily off the bone. But the calf feet also had another purpose. People were eating gelatin long before Jell-O became a household favorite. Even after commercial gelatin became available in stores, people agreed that homemade "jelly," as it was called, tasted better and was more nutritious. They made it by removing the skin and hooves from calves' feet, then boiling the feet to release their fatty gelatin. It took a lot of straining and careful heating, hot enough to liquefy it, but not hot enough to burn it. Four feet would yield a couple of quarts of clear liquid, which the cook then mixed with eggs, sugar, and spices. It could be flavored with anything from cinnamon to raspberries, strawberries, or persimmons, as well as almost any kind of fruits, nuts, and even cheese crumbles, and a good cook had a repertoire of various flavors of jellies. One of the most popular, especially in western Mississippi, was the tomato aspic. This odd, but festive, red mixture featured tomato juice, vinegar, and tiny chopped bits of celery and other vegetables suspended in the gelatin. It's still made today with lemon Jell-O, and considered by some Southerners to be the pinnacle of the culinary arts.

If Americans of today want turtle soup, they have to go to New Orleans, where it's still proudly served in a few fine restaurants, usually with a glass of sherry, which some people like to add to the soup. But from the earliest colonial times it was one of the most popular dishes in America, and was even part of the Campbell's Soup line as late as the 1920s. Any kind of turtle could be made into turtle soup, but it was so much work cleaning and butchering them, everybody wanted the biggest ones they could find, and that meant snapping turtles. Most people said they were the best tasting, and certainly provided the most meat, as they normally weighed over twenty pounds, and some over 100. It was said that a snapping turtle contained seven kinds of meat that had the taste and texture of chicken, beef, shrimp, veal, goat, fish, and pork. Once the meat was butchered, making turtle soup was pretty much like making any other soup. The meat was browned in butter, then vegetables and spices added, along with a roux. Grease was skimmed off of the mixture as it simmered for a long time, until most of the liquid was gone, and the result was a thick and chunky soup.

Turtle soup eventually fell victim to the fact

Turtle soup was once so popular that recipes abounded for mock turtle soup made from beef, chicken, and pork.

that it takes so much work to clean a whole turtle. Besides, turtle meat didn't lend itself to pretty cuts of meat packed in neat containers, the way steaks, roasts, and fish filets do. It comes off the animal in small bits and shreds that were more suitable to packing in cans. So as other meats became increasingly available in cans, as well as in grocery store refrigerator cases, turtle just didn't look very appetizing. After all, that was also a time when our society was raising generations of children who never learned to cut up the animals they were going to eat.

At one time, recipes abounded for mock turtle soup, using shreds of other meats in place of turtle meat in recipes for soups and stews. Why use beef or pork for mock turtle soup instead of simply calling it beef or pork soup? Just because turtle was so incredibly popular.

The most popular meat for mock turtle was on the head. One mid-1800s family recipe called, "Dress a Calf Head like a Turtle," instructed the cook, "Take a good calf head—leave the skin on—wash it in several waters 'till all the blood is out—drain it in a sieve and wipe it dry in a table cloth—dredge it with flour and season it with salt, mace, nutmeg, and cayenne—bake it two hours—add plenty gravy made from the bones." Mace is a very expensive spice made from outer coverings of the nutmeg nut, and has a lot more flavor than the ground spice. The recipe called for adding a handful of chopped parsley in a pint of wine, then another hour of baking, and it suggested serving the dish with forcemeat. Forcemeat is basically sausage without the spices, a mixture of meat, usually pork and fat, put through a grinder. The forcemeat was mixed with eggs and boiled, then offered as a side dish to the Mock Turtle Soup. That particular recipe added, "If the head is thin, it will require some butter."

Even aside from mock turtle dishes, calf and hog heads were prized for their tasty meat. The tough, stringy meat had to be tenderized, sometimes with milk, but more often with an acid like vinegar. But the most common tenderizer in old Southern recipes was wine. That might sound like a luxury, but for people who were gathering and preserving all sorts of fruit, it was normal to set some aside to ferment. It wasn't always very good drinking wine, but was always good in meat dishes.

Mincemeat was one of the most difficult and time-consuming dishes a cook could undertake. It could be made from pork or beef, and a lot of cooks agreed that the best mincemeat was made with the shreds scraped from a hog's head. The meat was mixed with suet, sometimes in equal parts, but some cooks made mincemeat with suet, and no meat at all. Recipes called for endless lists of ingredients, like citron, an imported fruit similar to lemon, but less acidic, and "a wine glass of rose water." Some recipes called for the feet of calves or pigs to be boiled, then the resulting jelly pushed through a colander, cooled, then heated and pushed through again, resulting in a lumpy gelatin that was said to look like "pearl barley." Then that was added to the meat mixture. The mixture was usually stored in a stone crock, sealed with butter, and kept in a cool place. To make mincemeat pies, a crust was spread over a shallow bowl, the mincemeat filling and a

top crust were added, and the pies were baked, then eaten hot or cold.

Later mincemeat recipes called for sirloin or other good, lean beef. But the original idea of mincemeat was to mix otherwise unusable shreds of meat with fruit, sugar, and alcohol. Sometimes three times as much alcohol as any other ingredient, which may have made mincemeat pies a lot more fun than they were palatable. As Andy Griffith, television's sheriff of Mayberry, once said, "Mincemeat without the brandy is downright sacrilegious!"

Today, with our concern about fat in the diet, it may be hard to imagine that suet was an important ingredient in American cooking until very recently. The early European immigrants brought recipes for suet puddings and suet dumplings, and they met Indians who ate pemmican, a mixture of suet, jerky, and fruit. Suet, the hard fat that grows around the kidneys and loins of cows and sheep, was preferred to butter and other fats in some pastries because it made them soft, as opposed to flakey. But the real reason it was so important in the South is because of the southern love for fried foods. Suet has a high melting point, and can be kept very hot for a

PORCH TALK

In the Boston Mountains of Arkansas, Pearl Moon Stanfield recalls the community aspect of using every part of an animal. If the family had more than they could use, they took the rest around to the neighbors, and somebody always wanted it. She says, "We just never know what somebody else needs until we offer."

A North Carolina woman renders lard from pork fat in a cast iron kettle over an open fire. (Courtesy of the Library of Congress)

Neighbors help with hog killing time in Virginia. The animals hang on a rack in the background, waiting to be butchered, with a fire smoldering near them to keep flies away. (Courtesy of Library of Congress.)

long time without smoking or burning. It was perfect for deep frying a long list of dishes like fried fish, fried pies, fried okra, fried green tomatoes, and of course, fried chicken. Lard is the pork equivalent of suet, made from the same kind of fat found around pig kidneys. Early farmers rendered their own lard, heating it with a little water to keep it from burning. When it was strained, it came out snow white and odorless, and was good for lots of recipes, including baking.

As long as there have been animals on the earth, people have eaten marrow, the juicy inside of big bones. It's power-packed stuff, loaded with iron. Ancient people ate it fresh from the bone, and later generations cooked it out, then added it to other foods. Europeans cut the backbone of large animal into sections, wrapped them in dough, and baked them. They also made loaves of marrow, and their recipes included marrow pudding, a blend of bread crumbs, eggs, brandy, sugar, with "a pound of marrow sliced from a loaf." Those immigrants enjoyed such dishes in the Old Country, but once they became Americans, and start showing off their newly-gained wealth, they turned up their noses at marrow and its derivatives, regarding them as poor people's food. Then when times got tough, especially in the years following the Civil War, some of those same people were thrilled to once again savor a slice of mother's bread slathered with a big spoonful of marrow chutney.

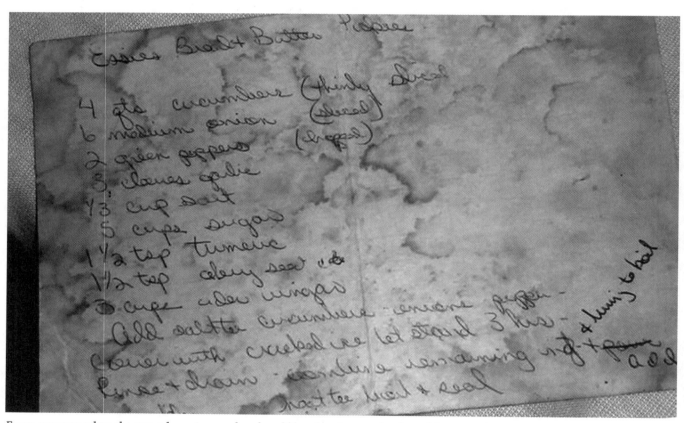

Essies Bread + Butter Pickles

4 qts cucumbers (thinly sliced)
6 medium onion (sliced)
2 green peppers (chopped)
3 clones garlic
⅓ cup salt
5 cups sugar
1½ tsp tumeric
1½ tsp celery seed &
3 cups cider vinegar
Add salt to cucumbers - onion - peppers -
Cover with cracked ice let stand 3 hrs -
Rinse + drain   combine remaining ing + bring to boil
heat tee boil + seal   add

Every summer, when the cucumbers ripen, a decades-old hand-written recipe for pickles gets a few more stains and notes.

Chapter 11

Pickling and Preserving

Old cookbooks have sizeable chapters on pickles and relishes. Of course, pickles are pickles, and they can be made from cucumbers and lots of other vegetables. Relishes, like Audrey Stanfield Asling's squash relish, with its cucumbers, onions, and peppers, were once a popular side dish on the everyday table. But pickling was about more than just a quaint garnish or a tangy topping; it was a method of preserving food. Folks pickled beef, beef tongue, fish, pork, cucumbers, okra, peppers, corn, onions, pig's feet, beets, tomatoes, cabbage, watermelon, cantaloupe, onions, cherries, blackberries, and walnuts. Also mushrooms, grapes, eggs, and apples. In the era before refrigerators and freezers, pickling was just one of the numerous and fascinating methods of preserving food, some of which continue today.

Hungry people couldn't always afford to be overly particular about what they were going to eat on any given day. Farmers never knew for sure which crops were going to come in, and which were going to disappear to heat, cold, or wildlife. They had to be ready to dry, smoke, salt, can, or pickle whatever they had. That way of thinking produced an era of American cooking from colonial days to well into the 20th century, which was nothing short of amazing in its level of adaptability and opportunism. Before the modern era of super stores and super highways, people couldn't just run to the corner and buy what they needed, and that was especially true for rural folks. For them, the stores were far away and the food was expensive. So it was really important to make food last for a week, a month, and even through the winter.

Dried herbs, peppers, and garlic hung in the kitchen rafters. An apple stored with the potatoes kept them from sprouting. Carrots and turnips could be kept tender and crisp by cutting the tops short, dipping both top and root in melted paraffin, then storing them in an old lard can. Folks used to dry beef, fish, turkey, venison, corn, apples, and grapes, which of course are still known by the old French name for grapes, raisins. They salted meat and whiskeyed peaches. They kept most root crops, onions, fresh fruits, and berries in the cool, dry root cellar, where the temperature was pretty constant. And if the house didn't have a cellar, a hole in the ground would do. The family would dig a hole big enough to hold a wooden or tin box, line it with straw, add a lid with two inches of sod on it, and the little cooler would keep a pretty steady temperature all year. It was a thrill for a child to come home from school on a chilly February day, open the box, and pull out a crisp apple she put in the box back in September. They kept milk, cream, butter, and cheese in the spring house, which was usually a little stone or wood shed with a shingle roof, built over the cool water coming out of a spring. Any dairy goodies placed in that box would stay refreshingly cool. In fact, a good spring house would keep the temperature pretty steady all year 'round because of the cool moving water. Even in winter, the stored food didn't freeze unless the spring froze completely.

In the 1800s the jars and lids for home canning were developed, with the most notable brand being the Ball Mason jar. To start canning from scratch required a fair investment in jars, lids, rubber rings to seal the lids, and in better equipped kitchens, a rack to hold the jars while they were being sterilized in boiling water. Those who couldn't afford the rack sterilized their jars with sunlight. The investment was expensive, but was such an essential part of life, both on the farm and in town, that families made sure they found a way to buy what they needed. Once a family had their supplies, they could be used repeatedly, year after year, replacing only the rubber rings. They canned corn, tomatoes, tomato juice, tomato sauce, applesauce, green beans, dilled beans, pinto beans, peas, black-eyed peas, peaches, beets, almost any kind of fruit, from cherries to peaches, as well as rhubarb, squash, and even greens like spinach and collards.

The Mason jar company still sells about seventy percent of its jars and lids to people in rural areas, which means more than a quarter of them are sold to the folks in town. So why would a modern city dweller go through all the work of canning green beans when they can go to the giant grocery store on the corner and buy green beans that were canned in a factory? For that matter, when rural families are stocking up on toilet paper and beer, why wouldn't they grab their green beans in tin cans too? First, the old methods still work. Second, the food tastes different and good, and the green beans are greener. Third, it goes hand in hand with raising and gathering fresh, healthy food at home without chemical additives, pesticides, or herbicides. And fourth, some people still enjoy doing the work and being part of the whole process of home food production. It simply feels good, especially when using grandma's jars, or the jar in which a best friend brought over some pepper jelly last Christmas.

Families also dried fruit, which was later brought back to life by boiling. Or they brandied it, which meant letting it ferment, in what was called a mélange. Bananas, grapes, and apples couldn't be used in brandied fruit, but cherries, peaches, pears, pineapple, raspberries, and strawberries all went in with plenty of sugar. The mélange was kept in a crock in a cool, dark place, and brought out to be used as a topping for puddings and desserts. An old letter describes another small-batch method of keeping fermented fruit:

My great-aunt in South Carolina kept a jar of fruit—all kinds—in some kind of fermented juice for years. It was always on the counter in the kitchen, every so often she'd throw something into it—cherries, plums, peaches, lemons, whatever was around—with some sugar, and stir it up. It was sweet, syrupy, and definitely had a kick. (Although great-aunt was a stout tee-totaler and vowed 'no likker, bahr, ner strong drank' came into her household!) She usually served it over vanilla ice cream or pound cake.

Even rotting fruit was put to use. Old slave interviews tell about how vinegar was made from apples, and how vinegar is just a few weeks removed from turning to wine and brandy. Millie Evans, of Arkansas, described making vinegar, saying, "We scooped up the apples and ground them up and put them in a sack and let them drip. Didn't add no water, and when it got done dripping, we let it sour

Water can be seen flowing below the floor of this Tennessee spring house, keeping the temperature about the same all year. Dairy products and other food were stored in the crocks and cans. (Courtesy of the Library of Congress)

Those who couldn't afford the pots and racks to sterilize their jars in boiling water had to sterilize them with sunlight, like these on a fence near Conway, AR. (Courtesy of the Library of Congress)

and let it stand, and had some of the best vinegar ever made." There were other methods, and one was about as easy as another. A gallon of molasses set in the sun for five weeks produced vinegar. It went a little faster with half molasses and half cider. Susan High, who was born into a North Carolina slave family, related, "There was lots of things to drink . . . cider, made from apples, whiskey, and brandy."

Some families still keep some vinegar in great grandma's cruet, and not only add vinegar to greens and cabbage as they're cooking, but also use it as a topping for greens and other dishes. Vinegar was historically so popular that by 1900 it had become a common condiment on American tables. It proved a perfect complement to the pork fat that was cooked into all kinds of vegetables, from broccoli to beets. Wrapping cheese in a vinegar cloth kept it fresh, and a few drops of vinegar while candy was cooking kept it creamy. People have found medicinal uses for vinegar for centuries, and the old cookbooks, which always had a chapter on household cleaning, listed vinegar as a dependable and easily replaceable cleaner. As one early homemaker wrote, "It got the windows so clean we were in danger of the goats jumping through them."

Deep in winter, farm wives would go to the cellar, where they kept their canned goods, and select a meat entrée from the jars of beef, wild game, fish, and chicken. Or they'd go to the shed with a hatchet or saw, and carve whatever was needed from the hanging, sometimes frozen, meats that had been salted, pickled, smoked, or dried the previous fall. None of that is particularly Southern, and in fact, most of the methods used by American farm families prior to 1900 had been used around the globe in one form or another since ancient times. Perhaps the world's oldest method of preserving meat is smoking,

simply letting it hang over a smoldering hickory fire day and night for weeks. Once smoked, it kept for months. Farms generally had a smoke house, built just for smoking and hanging meat through the winter. Some families preferred the relatively quick method of curing their pork by rubbing salt and sugar into it and letting it dry. After a month or two it was cured. The family might carve off enough for a big feast and hang the rest in the smoke house. Of all the methods of preserving meat, pickling was the least common, partly because it was so labor intensive, and partly because of the flavor it gave the meat. Still, people pickled not only pork, but also beef, mutton, oysters, and mussels. Former slave Mary Davis of Texas said of pickling beef, "We'd take a barrel with a good bottom in it,

PORCH TALK

Unlike cooking a delicious meal, and then sitting down to enjoy it, preserving food was a case of delayed gratification, a lot of work for a distant reward. Folks in Alabama tell about a man who wanted to remove a sapling from beside his cabin door. But he decided his axe was too big for such a little tree. So he waited and waited for it to be the right size. Finally, he got accustomed to the sapling, and didn't even notice it as he walked by every day. Then one day he started to leave the cabin and "clunk." The little sapling had grown into a massive tree with a trunk so thick it blocked the door. By then, his axe was truly too big, and he couldn't swing it in the space that was left, so he had to tear down the cabin.

They say things will never be exactly as we want them to be. So do the canning, pickling, smoking, curing, and cutting the tree, today for a happy tomorrow.

then put chunks of raw meat into it. We'd mix some salt with some saltpeter. Then we'd put a mixture of that on the bottom." Actually, the saltpeter is optional. All that's required is about a gallon of salt for 100 pounds of meat. Some folks like the flavor of adding about four pounds of brown sugar. That type of pickling is called salting. If the meat is packed in liquid, it's called brining. A crock was used instead of a barrel, there had to be enough salt in the water that an egg will float, and the meat must be completely covered in the brine. Once the meat was packed, the crock or barrel was covered and kept cool, usually in a cellar. Then once a week the meat was taken out, the brine was stirred, and the meat was replaced. At three weeks, the meat was edible, and at the end of four weeks it was done. Before the brine thickened and spoiled, homemakers had to take the pickled meat out and pack it in jars or dry crocks, where it would keep for months. Old timers were quick to point out that if the meat floats, it must be held down by a plate with a rock on it, or as Mary Davis said, "Some rocks was put on top."

Preserving food took a sharp turn with the popularity of the ice box, the early refrigerator, which kept food cool with blocks of ice. After about 1870, everybody who was anybody in the cities had one of those, and an ice man drove his wagon around town, delivering the ice right to the box. But in the country, there was no reason to buy an ice box if the family couldn't get ice for it. When the ice box finally caught on in the South in the 1900s, electric power wasn't far behind, and the refrigerator made it possible to keep produce, meat, and dairy goods handy. Yet, in the South, more than any other part of the country, people continued to can and pickle and dry and smoke their food, for two reasons. First, because it tastes so good. And second, all those preserving methods are woven into the fabric of southern social life.

Chapter 12

Stirring the Southern Pot

Over about four centuries, several American ports have hosted immigrants coming to the New World from Europe. Germans and Scots-Irish were entering the country through New York and Philadelphia as early as the 1700s. The British colonists landed in several places, with Boston emerging as the first true major port city. Then Irish immigration spiked in the 1840s, coinciding with the potato famine in Ireland. It was also a time the poor could get cheap passage on American cotton ships returning from Europe to New Orleans. Germans liked America's cities, dairy farms, crafts, cheese-making, and cold weather, and they brought with them a fierce spirit of nationalism, so they quickly became passionate American patriots. During the Civil War they were staunchly Unionist, and some Union Army regiments were composed entirely of Germans. Baltimore grew as a point of entry, and Boston became increasingly popular among the Irish.

New Orleans was the most active Southern port, but the accumulation of silt almost stopped navigation in the late 1800s. Galveston was popular, especially after the Civil War, but was wiped out by a hurricane in 1900, so travelers returned to the newly-rebuilt port of New Orleans. The California Gold Rush started in 1849, not only drawing Americans from the East to travel by wagon, but also attracting Europeans. Some of them entered eastern ports and then traveled west, while others sailed around South America to San Francisco. During that entire time, swirling numbers of different cultures entered the young nation, and though they tended to stick together with their kinsmen and ethnic groups for security and mutual support, as much as to preserve and enjoy their language and cultures, they also interacted, owned businesses, taught schools, and otherwise mingled in public, contributing their unique views and styles of living to the emerging American way of life.

The nation's first 150 or so years of immigration was important to the way the Civil War divided the culture of home and family. By far, most of the immigrants settled in the North. Then Southern ports were blockaded during the Civil War, so no new immigrants came into the South, and even after the war, it took years to rebuild Southern ports and restore emigration to the Southern states. Most of the rails and riverboats were in the North, and newcomers were attracted to the promise of the American West, including free land for homesteading, the trans-continental railroad, and gold and silver strikes, which kept appearing from 1849 to the 1890s. Compared to much of the rest of America, the entire South was somewhat isolated, with few people moving in for several decades. With little new ethnic influence, Southerners became increasingly Americanized, losing their old European ways, and evolving their own uniquely Southern culture. Meanwhile, Northern cities, factories, and ethnic strongholds, along with the continued stream of Europeans, meant the North retained and strengthened its European roots.

The differences between North and South can be seen as distinctly in death as in life. Today, Southern drivers, especially in small towns, pull over and stop while a funeral procession passes by. It's not required by law, but shows respect and quietly shares in the family's grief. In the North, it's almost unheard of. And that's part of the broader story of evolving Southern traditions, in contrast to Northern and Eastern people clinging to older ethnic traditions. When someone in the family died, many Americans followed some of the Old World rules, like covering the mirrors, stopping the clocks, getting the deceased into the ground quickly, and in the Jewish tradition, no cut flowers, which would symbolize cutting the cycle of life and growth. Meanwhile, in the South, the passing of a loved one was increasingly marked with music, celebration, and an evolving blend of observations. The Irish wake, calling for sitting up and drinking alcohol all night with the corpse in the parlor, became far less formal in the South. Slave songs and spirituals mixed with Baptist hymns to create a new role for church music, as people enjoyed the emotional release of communal singing. That meant, at funerals, the songs steadily became more important, not to mention louder and more celebratory. In New Orleans, mourners organized "second lines," raucous brass-band parades that played everything from dirges to ragtime favorites, while the crowd danced in the streets wearing colorful outfits. White people gradually adopted African-American customs that would have once been considered superstitious, like decorating graves with not only heaping mounds of flowers, but also mementos, pictures, and dolls. Those practices led to the illustrated grave markers of today that feature all kinds of memorials, including slick engravings of helicopters and running shoes, photos preserved on porcelain medallions, and recordings of the deceased person's voice. All of that is more common in the South. And while people throughout history have been buried with personal treasures, just as ancient Vikings were buried with weapons, funeral directors report that it's becoming increasingly popular in the modern South. People have been buried with everything from a golf ball in their pocket to a watermelon and a six-pack of beer.

But above all, the South remains the stronghold of greeting and defeating death with food. It's a direct result of the Reconstruction experience, where every hardship was diminished by gratitude, hope, and celebration of divine provision. It's a declaration that we may be hurting, but we'll get through this too. That's why, at the first word of someone's passing, people organize with military precision to provide meals for the family. There's the mountain of food brought to the home, then the "repast," a big meal served for the family at the church, generally right before the funeral service. And if the deceased and their loved ones attended different churches, both churches pitch in. Friends come by to serve and clean up the kitchen, and volunteer to take care of the babies during the funeral. They bring cakes, pies, and an unending procession of casseroles. The food tastes good, feels good, brings smiles and laughter, and ignites the telling and retelling of old stories that often begin with,

"Your daddy and I go way back." In the South, people in mourning have learned that the love and community of preparing and sharing food is a blessing that works hand-in-hand with the pastor's assurance that life goes on.

That unfolding story of the post-Civil War South, and how it differed from the rest of the country, was simply a continuation of what had been happening in the half-century before 1860. When the Civil War came along, Kansas was just entering the Union. Nebraska and the great sprawling plains, Rocky Mountains, and Sierra Madres, were a vast wilderness inhabited by Native Americans. European Americans had been prowling around the West, trapping, trading, and taking freight along the Santa Fe Trail, from Kansas City to the border with Mexico. After the Louisiana Purchase in 1803, migrants started their journey from St. Louis, up the Missouri River to the great Northwest. St. Louis was both a destination and a departure point, so all the arriving Easterners gave it a continued Eastern flavor.

It's understandable that after the Civil War Yankees weren't yearning to move into Confederate strongholds like Virginia and the Deep South. But they did move into Missouri, Kentucky, Arkansas, and Texas. Those states still had strong southern traditions, but the Border States in particular were viewed by many, including Union Army veterans as a sort of conquered Yankee territory, with plenty of available government land, and small, vacant family farms up for sale. And wherever the Yankees moved, they brought with them Yankee cooking traditions. Various national and ethnic groups had been simmering in the American melting pot, where their recipes were adopted by their fellow Americans and adapted to the New World. The Irish had long crowned their shepherd's pie with creamy potatoes, but in the South, it may have been topped with cornmeal mush. Germans had the Lutheran Church, cheese, and bratwurst, while Scots, Jews, and Eastern Europeans made haggis and kishke, their respective versions of stuffed intestines. All those sausages needed fillers, so in America, if oats weren't available, it was rice or barley, ground nuts, or the trusted cornmeal. And for spices, sausage makers used everything from wild garlic and sage to peppergrass and wild rose. Yankees turned Missouri grasslands into prime beef and dairy country, and that's how Myrtle Branson, living in the western part of the state, came to make brown gravy, which the family called Yankee gravy. The southern tradition was to make cream gravy, with chicken fat or lard, plus cream, while Yankees, with a better supply of beef, made their brown gravy with beef drippings. Myrtle's family hated it, so any time she made it, she'd also whip up some good southern cream gravy.

The brown or white gravy debate was a perfect example of the ongoing culinary conversation about fats. Southerners loved their pork fat and lard. Yankees loved milk, cheese, and butter. Union Army veteran Henry Bailey brought his wife Hannah from Indiana to homestead in Missouri in 1867. Like every other family, they kept a cow for milk, butter, and cheese. On churning day, Hannah would scoop fresh butter into her press, and push out perfect, round, yellow blocks, each stamped with a swimming swan. For the price of a sack of cornmeal they would have the cow bred about once a year, and then the family would have a calf to trade or butcher. Traditional Northern thinking called for making sure they never ran out of butter. That was less critical for southern families. They liked their butter too, but if they ever ran out, they were happy with a little bacon grease on their biscuits.

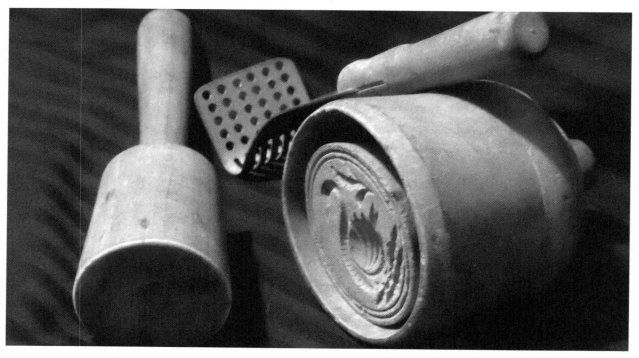

Hannah Bailey's prized swan butter mold, pictured with her potato masher and a wooden pestle.

The process of making butter was more complex than it would appear, with lots of options, and it required time, plus a good bit of artistry and experience. Fresh milk could be strained through a cloth and drunk right from the cow, but some people didn't like it warm, so they cooled it in the spring house. Nobody could drink much of it because it was too rich with cream. So they let some of the milk sit at warm temperatures, and it would begin to form balls, called clabber, which could be strained off, and hung in a cloth with a little salt added, letting the water drip out, leaving something like cottage cheese.

To make butter, folks let the milk sit for a few hours or even overnight, while the sweet cream rose to the top. They had to watch it carefully, because if it sat too long, it became sour cream. Once it separated, they skimmed the cream off with a skimmer, which was a thin-edged, wooden saucer, or a metal skimmer with holes in the bottom to let the milk drain out. Except for a bit that might have been set aside for cooking, the cream went into the churn. The classic model was a plunger that had some sort of blades or paddle on it and was pumped up and down in a jar. The sizes varied from big ones that sat on the floor between the feet to little table-top models, and in the late 1800s lots of new ones came to market, with metal gears and cranks to make churning easier.

The churning took thirty minutes to an hour, and depended on a number of factors, including the temperature. The results were unpredictable, so it's no wonder that superstitions and family traditions developed around churning, like throwing some salt on the hearth before starting. If a guest came by, they were expected to take a turn with the churning. If they didn't, it was commonly believed they would take the butter with them, and it would never form. But if all went well, the yellow butter gradually formed balls, then clumps, then could be taken out, and it still had to be put in a cloth and the water pressed out of it. Buttermilk was the sour liquid left after making butter. Some folks liked to drink it, and everybody liked buttermilk biscuits.

There's plenty of butter and plenty of fat in the Southern diet, but our cooking was intended to be eaten by hard-working people who burn a lot of fuel in their furnace. The way Southerners see it, cholesterol, butter, and fat never killed anybody, because everybody also ate a balanced diet and worked hard. Elias Stanfield, for example, ate a fried egg every morning of his life, mowed the grass with a reel push mower until he was well into his nineties, and lived to be 102.

Beef, buffalo, and bear fat could all be used in cooking, but in the South, pork fat was the pinnacle of the grease world. Everything from

Young Michael Barham helps his Grandmother, Mama Ruth, with the churning in Cass, AR. Behind them can be seen a fairly new addition to the kitchen, a sink that drained to the back yard. (Courtesy of Michael Barham)

eggs to greens was fried in pork grease, and lots of dishes, from pinto beans to squash casserole, started with browning a chunk of salt pork, then cutting it up and stirring it back in. Baking pans were greased by rubbing with salt pork. Grease, milk, and cornmeal went into making cornmeal gravy. Fresh green beans were snapped, then simmered in water and bacon grease until they were so soft they were falling apart. Today, baked potatoes are often actually microwaved potatoes, ready with the push of a button, and served to people who eat the insides, but throw out the tough skins. It's a reflection of America's pressure cooker mentality that even when we're not in a hurry, we fix and eat our food as if we are. But the traditional Southern way to bake potatoes or sweet potatoes is to rub the skins with bacon grease, put them in a pan, and bake them at a medium temperature for about an hour. The skins of both kinds of potatoes are rich in fiber and other nutrients, and sweet potato skins, which few people eat today, are packed with iron and beta carotene. When they're greased and baked, the skins come out chewy and delicious. Collards, spinach, turnip, and mustard greens were all cooked in bacon or salt pork grease and water. Some cooks added a little sliced onion. And the most common way to cook greens is with judicious amounts of salt, red pepper, cider vinegar, and just enough sugar to make the kids like them.

A few years after the Civil War was over, and the ports of Louisiana, Florida, Virginia, and the Carolinas reopened, Southerners could again enjoy the imported foods they had before the years of scarcity and depredation. Cooks clamored for black tea, white sugar, wheat, oranges, lemons, cinnamon, black pepper, vanilla, nutmeg, and allspice. As more people moved in and out of the South, with good roads and rails carrying more of them to more places, Southern cooking became even more diverse. Southern cooks got their hands on new dishes and adapted them to what they knew and to the ingredients they had on hand. Gradually, foods like pineapples and bananas returned to market.

Bananas had once been imported from the Caribbean, and had been popular throughout the young United States. However, they ripened and spoiled quickly, before they could be consumed in the Northern portions of the country, and that's why the South was the main American consumer of bananas, both before and after the Civil War. In fact, a banana plantation was started in Florida in 1876, but it soon failed because the temperature wasn't consistently warm enough. So bananas were destined to remain an import, and with the low cost of island labor, they were affordable for almost everyone. Their acid content is so low that they can't safely be canned, but they were added to other canned foods, like banana-currant preserves and banana-strawberry jam. And since they have such a short shelf life, it's not surprising that cooks, especially those in the South, found delicious ways to use them. A soft banana could be blended into almost any cake. And the two big favorites came to be banana pudding and banana nut bread, both of which are made with bananas that are past their prime eating stage, and both of which are still Southern icons today.

Banana pudding can trace its roots to layered deserts like the English trifle, a liquor-soaked pound cake at the bottom of a bowl, topped with fruit, then custard, then fruit, and sometimes more layers of custard and fruit. Custard, a creamy, baked mix of eggs, cream, sugar, and vanilla, was a natural complement to bananas. But Southern cooks vastly preferred something lighter than pound cake, so when they made a trifle, pound cake was replaced by lady fingers or sponge cake. The liquor disappeared, simply as a matter of Southern taste. Over time, cooks shifted the true taste of the dish from the tangy liquored cake to the sweet banana mixture. During the same period, Southerners were developing a love for pudding, a simple mix of milk, sugar, and cornstarch, with almost any fruit flavoring. So it was a natural change from the custard, which used a lot of precious eggs, to comparatively cheap pudding. Vanilla wafers were introduced by Nabisco in the 1920s, and they were not only handy and easier than baking lady fingers or sponge cake for the bottom of the pan, but they were also cute and decorative perched around the edges of the pan. They seemed to say, "Look at this fun and colorful desert." But the overriding reason banana pudding became a Southern favorite is because, like many Southern dishes, it lends itself to big social gatherings. A pie, after all, is a pie, and will only yield so many pieces. Cookies are individual treats; they're not communal. A banana pudding is easier and quicker than a cake, it shows up at the church dinner or wedding party in a big pan, and it can be dished up in as many large or small portions as needed to fit the crowd. And maybe the biggest reason of all that Naner Puddin' is so loved in the South, is that after a day in the hot, Southern sun, followed by a big meal of spicy gumbo or sauce-dripping barbecue, it's a cool treat that feels good in the mouth.

North Carolina's Fanny McKinney Stanfield used a banana nut bread recipe with a tiny, but powerful secret ingredient, a mere two tablespoons of applesauce. Again, one of the common ways of making apples last into the winter was to turn them into applesauce, so there was almost always some applesauce on the shelf in the root cellar. That little addition to Fanny's banana nut bread was moist, tasty,

decidedly Southern, and decidedly delicious. Or maybe it's the fact that her recipe specified that the bananas must be mashed with a wooden spoon. Either way, her method is now gracing Southern tables in at least its fourth generation.

Myrtle Branson, the one who made both Yankee gravy and cream gravy, moved with her family in a covered wagon from Missouri to Texas in 1896, and on the wagon train she met her future husband, William Franklin Simpson. When those families migrated to the Gulf Coast, they had to learn a whole new way of life. After living for decades in the dry, rolling plains of Central Missouri, they relocated to Port Arthur, Texas, and their harvest, cooking, and taste buds all made an abrupt change from Missouri pork and corn to Texas fish and rice. They were poor, but they were also brave and adaptable, the kind of people who were reshaping the American South.

William Franklin Simpson and his brothers became professional fishermen, and along with their successful business, kept their family stocked with fish, crabs, and other treasures from the Gulf. They gave the children the job of separating the crabs. Any that were sickly or dead were thrown out, and the littlest ones were set aside. The women would chop vegetables, mix in some crab meat, and boil it down to gumbo. They fixed crabs in one way after another, from simple boiling to recipes that had to be followed to the letter.

According to legend, the dressing we enjoy with our Thanksgiving turkey started in France. It was a fairly common bread-based side dish that lent itself to the inclusion of all kinds of vegetables. The basic ingredients were crumbled bread, vegetables, and broth, whatever meat was on the stove, turkey, chicken, beef, or pork, providing the broth. It was after the Civil War, with President Lincoln's newly-created national holiday of

In 1896, the Branson family moved from Missouri to the Texas Coast. Wearing the bonnet in the center is Myrtle Branson, who met her future husband, William Franklin Simpson, on the wagon train. (Courtesy of Tanya Touchstone)

Thanksgiving, in which dressing became closely identified with turkey. And in the South, as with many dishes, the way people made it depended on what was at hand. If there was celery, great. If there was no celery, that was okay too. If there was an apple, it was added. If it didn't turn out pleasing to the cook, or the cook's loved ones, the next dressing was made a little different.

Even when a dish like dressing had humble beginnings, Southern cooks were like world-class hunting dogs, chasing down perfection, never settling, but always striving to make it the best it could be, and that's how dressing took on a life of its own. Frugal cooks—and all Southern cooks were frugal cooks—hated to throw out anything, and they were always looking for a way to reconstitute, disguise, add to, and otherwise use leftovers. Southern cooks might have wheat bread on hand, but they were sure to have cornbread, so this made cornbread the obvious and more frequent choice for dressing. Besides, when cornbread

is left over, it dries out quickly, and dressing was a good way to put dry cornbread to use. So that's how cornbread dressing became so popular in the South, as opposed to the traditional European wheat bread dressing.

Pearl Cole Davies was born and raised in DeRidder, Louisiana, and married a soldier from Detroit, who was born and raised in Wales. Pearl had to learn to cook Yankee rump roast and Yorkshire pudding for her husband, but she never wavered from her Louisiana Thanksgiving staple, cornbread-rice dressing. Her recipe began with sautéing celery and green onions in butter with salt and pepper. While it was cooking, she broke up a double batch of cornbread, added the cooked vegetables and four cups of broth. Then, straight from the heart of Louisiana, came three cups of cooked rice. But the real difference is that she added ham, collards, and pecans. That combination of ingredients gave Pearl's dressing a rainbow of tastes and a symphony of textures.

Dressing might include chestnuts, raisins, and mushrooms. There's giblet dressing, using the chopped heart, liver, and gizzard of the turkey. Families have nearly come to blows over oyster dressing; they either love it or hate it. So on special occasions, it wasn't uncommon for oyster dressing to share the table with another variety, just to keep peace, just like brown gravy and cream gravy.

Over time, the best dishes bubbled to the top, and Southern food got better because of standardization. Over the decades, more cooks got more utensils, including measuring cups and measuring spoons, and wood stoves with thermometers, so they were able to follow recipes more precisely, which made it easier for young cooks to learn how to make Granny's dishes. The South also built more roads leading to more stores on more corners. Families who once ate no white flour at all were able to buy it at the local store, and more branded merchandise was coming onto the market all the time. Campbell, Heinz, and Borden were selling canned foods in the 1870s. Arbuckle coffee was on the shelves before 1880, and Maxwell House appeared in Nashville in 1892. People increasingly lived near town, or in town, making it easier to buy canned goods to supplement their home-canned foods. If their peach crop was poor, they could buy canned peaches. All those changes happened first in Northern stores and homes, and little by little, they made their way into Southern homes. And all of that contributed to a nation of cooks who could replicate or change good recipes with predictable results.

Another prime contributor to more standard methods and predictable results in more kitchens was the emergence of cookbooks. During the late 1800s, the upshot in public education, and an improving Southern economy, meant everybody could read and write, which meant more homes had books, including cookbooks, on the shelf. That helped revive and preserve older methods and ingredients, and yet, like virtually all books of the time, early cookbooks were edited, published, and distributed in Northern cities like New York, Philadelphia, and Chicago. That meant the cookbooks had a decidedly Northern slant to which recipes they included and how the dishes were prepared. Then, in a second generation of publishing, specialized cookbooks emerged for Southern dishes, individual states, famous homes and plantations, along with collections of recipes from towns, churches, and the wives of military leaders and legislators. Not only were

PORCH TALK

For decades, from the late 1800s to the 1940s, cookbooks had entire chapters on "cooking for the sick." It was important, because hospitals were scarce, and only the most severe cases went there, while the sick were far more often nursed at home. After the Civil War and World War I, veterans with lost limbs and lingering wounds of all sorts grew older and had special needs. They might have been unable to work, take care of their homes, and raise, hunt, and gather their own food, and they surely couldn't afford to pay someone to do all that for them. There were none of today's assisted living facilities, and few old folks' homes. So when people grew old and infirm, or were otherwise sick, it was usually friends and family who cared for them. That's just what people did. In those days, almost everyone had to learn how to recognize maladies, change bandages, and otherwise take care of the ones in need, including cooking special meals for those with poor digestion and bad teeth. And it was all right there in the cookbook.

we becoming a nation of better cooks, but more of the secrets of Southern Cookin' were being preserved and replicated more precisely than ever before.

After the Civil War, literacy was higher in the North, particularly among women, but little girls in the South gradually joined the ranks of those who could read recipes and write their own. Education among former slaves, their children, and their grandchildren, meant they were preserving and sharing more of their recipes. It was also a time when the nation had outgrown some of its standards of civilized behavior, then further shattered them in war. So cookbooks provided instructions on how to set a table, and entire chapters on how to decorate a home, how to clean house, how to dress, and how to be polite. Those standards were always important in the South, where they suffered more from the war and its aftermath. As time went by, and as life has improved, those links to the proper aspects of Southern antebellum glory have proved to be vital not only to family identity, but to Southern style and culture in general. Even if the family never looked up the rules, those cookbooks carried an unspoken message in that decor and decorum are as important to home life as good eating. People found that it doesn't cost any money to be polite, and in spite of their hard times, their dignity and desire for civil living never faded, but grew ever stronger.

Still, with the world's cookbooks available today at the click of a button, some cooks still use the old hand-written recipes, or the ones that were typed on cute, store-bought cards, or the ones that had to be recopied because they'd become unreadable with tatters and stains. Through them, long ago cooks reach out to help one more time with their personal notes, stern instructions, and heartfelt blessings that transcend time and passing generations. Fanny McKinney Stanfield's banana nut bread recipe called for baking at 350 degrees, but she wrote an asterisk and a footnote, "I prefer a temperature around 325." The Simpsons' daughter-in-law Milly became famous along the Gulf Coast for her Smothered Crab recipe, which starts with an admonition, "Be sure to follow the recipe as near as possible." It's written in stream of consciousness, as she says, "Oh! Yes!" put the roux in the pot before the crabs, and "Oh! Yes!" drop a couple of bay leaves in the gravy. After all the work of cooking the crabs, she ends with the loving, "Then eat over rice and think of me."

Chapter 13

Cast Iron Skillets Sizzlin'

Ask almost any Southern cook to name the most essential Southern Cookin' utensil, the one thing they can't do without, and they'll say it's the iron skillet. This holy implement can be mishandled, abused, scraped, sanded, dropped from a covered wagon, overheated, unwashed, and left for dead to rust in the forgotten corner of a falling-down barn with a leaky roof. And a hundred years later some prophet of the kitchen can come along and breathe the breath of life into it, and it will live again, a stove-top Lazarus.

In 18th and early 19th century America, cast iron pots had a wire handle so they could hang on an arm that swung in and out of the fireplace, and skillets had three legs, so they could be set directly into the coals or on uneven hearth stones. Some pots had both a wire handle and legs. Then the kitchen stove revolutionized American cooking, and as stoves became widely available and affordable in the last half of the century, manufacturers started making cookware in more styles with flat bottoms, and no legs, so they could sit on the stove top.

Into that setting, the venerable cast iron skillet was born. It can be used to fry meat and eggs or sauté greens, and hardcore cooks get that special little shiver up their spine when cornbread's baking in it. To make cornbread, the secret is to heat the skillet first, then take it out of the oven, grease it well, and pour in the batter. Stick it back in the oven, and in fifteen minutes, it'll be cornbread.

Cast iron skillets and pots were the original non-stick pans. A well-seasoned skillet will easily release the food that's cooked in it, even eggs and sticky casseroles, but a cook who's going to be successful with cast iron has to follow a few rules. It must never be cleaned with soap if it can be cleaned with simple hot water and scrubbing. Nowadays stuck-on food can be loosened with a nylon scrubber, but for centuries dishwashers got by with a dish towel, a wooden spoon, and now and then, a fingernail. Almost any kind of food comes right off. If something tough like eggs gets cooked so hard it seems to have taken root in the iron, it just needs enough water to cover the bottom, heated to a boil, and the stuck-on food will scrub right out. If water alone doesn't do it, a little wood ashes or sand can be used to scrub the pan clean, although if it's sanded it has to be reseasoned. These ebony beauties can be seasoned over and over again, and they'll stand up to the passage of time much better than the cooks do.

They mustn't be scratched with metal utensils. Metal goes right through the seasoning, which is the non-stick coating, and then everything will stick to it. So wood utensils, and more recently plastic ones, have been used exclusively with cast iron. And cast iron isn't the best choice for long simmering

The cast iron skillet is in all its glory when it's baking corny cornbread.

of high-acid foods, like tomato sauces. The acid will cook off the seasoning, and then everything will stick. Cast iron mustn't be left on a hot stove with nothing in it, or the seasoning will dry out, and of course then food will stick. Even worse, if it gets too hot with nothing in it, the bottom can warp, and it'll never sit flat on the stove again.

Those are the do not's. There's also a list of do's. Cast iron must *always* be cleaned right after it's used. If food is left in it, the pan will rust. Just like food, if water is left sitting in it, the cast iron will rust. In fact, some folks say they can watch a dry, unseasoned pan rust right before their eyes, just from the moisture in the air. After it's washed, it has to be dried thoroughly, first with a towel, then by sitting on a warm, not hot, stove. If it gets too hot, the seasoning will dry out. So as soon as grandma

used her cast iron, she washed it, dried it on the stove over low heat, gave it a new thin coat of grease, put the lid on, and set it aside. If she stacked an iron pot inside another iron pot, she always put a rag between them because wherever they touch, they'll rust.

Does it sound like a lot to remember? Not if that's the way you've learned, and the way you've always cooked, and your mom and dad cooked, and your grandma and grandpa cooked, and so on. Cast iron is the only cookware that's so easy to take care of and will last virtually forever. It's almost impossible to break, it can't be dented, and cooks all across the South are still using iron pots that have been in their family for generations.

Of course, cast iron is really, really heavy. And interestingly, the weight of cast iron has a connection to the history of household architecture. There were hardly any built-in shelves, cabinets, or closets in 19th century American homes. The most modern and well-appointed plantation homes had massive kitchens, and in some cases the kitchen was in a separate building, which kept both the house and kitchen cooler in summer, and was a way to protect the house if there was ever a kitchen fire. But for most common folks, the kitchen was just a corner of the dining room. In fact, the great room design that's so popular today, was the way a lot of people lived, with one big room that served as the kitchen, sitting room, and dining room. But none of them, large or small, had much built-in storage. Instead, there were wardrobes for clothes, hutches for dishes, and china cabinets for fine glassware and serving pieces. The cooking pots, including heavy cast iron pieces, sat on the stove or hung from pegs on the wall or the rafters, and space was very limited. The more cookpots and utensils a cook had, the greater the storage problem. Gradually, the idea of kitchen cabinets emerged, along with clothes closets, in the 20th century, and cooks finally had some sturdy storage for cookware. They could have more pots and pans, and their weight really didn't matter.

During the 1800s, there were a lot of people on the move, and the weight of their belongings mattered a lot, especially for families moving west, who could only haul so much in their wagons and on horseback. It was customary for them to whittle their cookware down to something as simple as one skillet and one small boiling pot. Then in 1876 the cold handle skillet was patented. It was the most successful in the line of "single piece" skillets. This remarkable innovation was stamped from a sheet of steel, and the handle was wrapped in a separate piece of thin steel, with a slim air space between the layers

that kept it cool. The porous metal allowed it to be seasoned, giving it a non-stick surface,

PORCH TALK

Cast iron cookware can be seasoned and reseasoned as often and as many times as necessary. The first step in seasoning is to make sure there's no rust. If there's just a little spot of rust, it can usually be cleaned off and the rest of the coating can be left on. Even if a pan becomes badly rusted, the rust can be removed with a metal scrubber, and if that doesn't get it, then a wire brush, and if that still doesn't get it, sandpaper. The whole pan can be taken down to the bare metal, but that's rarely necessary. The traditional instructions on reseasoning are to wash the pan with soap and water and thoroughly dry it on a warm, not hot, stove. Then rub it with grease. Bacon grease will work, but lard is best. And put it upside down on a cookie sheet in an oven at 350 degrees. It's a good idea to take it out after a few minutes, when the grease is liquefied, and wipe the grease around so it makes a nice even coating, then put the pan back in the oven. After an hour, take it out and let it cool, then repeat the process. Three coats are good, but four or five may be better. Then the first time it's used after seasoning, the first thing cooked in it should be something good and greasy, like bacon. After that, pour the grease out, wipe the pan, and put it away until the next time it's needed.

While other cookware, especially those with modern non-stick coatings, will wear out, get scratched and dented, and need to be replaced, the more a cast iron pan is used, the better the seasoning becomes. The seasoning cooks onto and into the pores of the iron, becoming ever-so-slightly thicker and tougher, and making food slide more and more easily off. Many a Southern preacher has pointed out that the sweet irony of cast iron cookware is much the same with people. The more heat we go through, the less things stick to us.

just like good cast iron. Inventors tried all sorts of variations, and most of them were only variations, not improvements. Most had the handle riveted on, and some were quite beautiful, made of copper with tin linings. Copper conducts heat very well, so the copper pan heats evenly, without hot spots. But acid reacts with the copper, so dishes containing ingredients like tomatoes and vinegar can turn poisonous. Poison pans can give a cook a very bad reputation, and that's why such pans were lined with tin.

Light-weight pots and pans were a welcome addition to any kitchen, and yet they became most popular in the west, while Southerners, with their traditions of frugality and practicality, have never loosened their grip on their durable cast iron. They hung onto their wooden spoons too. Why wooden spoons? Partly because metal utensils scratch the seasoning on cast iron pots and pans. But also because wooden spoons are made of handy, replaceable hardwood, and if they wear out or break, a new spoon is as close as the woodpile, just waiting to be whittled out of a log.

There was a time when a man with a saw, chisel, hammer, pocket knife, and file could make almost anything from wood. Carving knives with concave blades would scoop the insides out of a bowl or spoon. Wooden bowls were wiped with a light coat of grease every time they were washed, which kept them from cracking, and kept flavors and juices from soaking in. If a wooden handle broke on anything on the place, they'd replace that right away. To save space and weight when people

This hand-made copper skillet is lined with tin, and features a long handle that's both riveted and soldered.

moved across country, they'd sometimes leave their handles behind, take the tool heads, and make new handles when they arrived. Of course, a lucky family moving into a home often found a ready bunch of handles waiting for them on the porch. If a family had a fire that burned the handles of their tools or kitchen utensils, the heads were salvaged and fitted with new handles. Edged tools, like axes, chisels, hammers, and knives, could lose their temper in a fire. But the craftsman could just build a hot fire, heat the heads, plunge them into cool water, then back into the fire, then back into the water, and they'd be re-tempered. Then they were ready to take a new edge and go back to work.

Even the poorest homes had a mortar and pestle, and some well-equipped cooks had both a wooden set and another set made of stone. As fortunes improved, families turned to the local general store for new and improved kitchen labor savers like the coffee grinder, potato masher, nut chopper, meat grinder, apple peeler, cabbage shredder, can opener, and graters in various sizes. But even today, some Cherokee and other native people still use a traditional thigh-high wooden pestle to crush peppers, seeds, nuts, corn, and almost every kind of spice.

Even through the hardest of times, some families held tight to their fine household goods. As they set their tables with heirloom, hand-painted dishware, they added such special pieces as the bone dish, a little place for each person to put their chicken and fish bones. The gravy separator kept the gravy's skin from pouring onto the mashed potatoes. The well-set table included a mustard jar, a spoon holder with enough spoons for everyone, and individual salt cellars at each seat, each with a tiny spoon. The centerpiece was the cruet set, usually a rack made of silver or other metal, with a handle, and it held stoppered condiment bottles. Most sets featured oil and vinegar, along with pepper sauce, ketchup, lemon juice, or other favorites of the family. So today, when we see salt and pepper and a bottle of ketchup on the table at a restaurant, we're looking at a long-standing American tradition.

Around 1880, American companies started manufacturing both pressed glass, which was made in cast iron molds, and cut glass, in which patterns were cut by hand using grinding wheels and files. Both were heavy and sturdy, both featured beautiful, intricate patterns, and both were very affordable. So while the wealthy set their tables with fine china and crystal, the great rising middle class set their tables with everything, including dinner plates, made of pressed or cut glass. Serving bowls and platters, candy dishes, and other incidentals became popular gifts, ushering in a new era of elegance for hard-working Americans, a trend that lasted until World War I. In fact, because the South has always been less trendy, and has clung tighter to touches that brighten the difficulties of everyday life, pressed and cut glass were even more precious, were popular longer, and enjoyed a stronger tradition of gifting and bequeathing among Southern families. In Appalachia, where money for gifts is hard to come by, a tradition evolved of

PORCH TALK

It was said that wooden spoons are like people. Put them to work, and the strong ones hold up. If they wear out, maybe that was the wrong spoon for the job.

This cut-glass spoon holder sat in the middle of the table, always full of spoons for the next meal. The owner painted the flowers to add color to the table.

bringing a small short cake as a wedding gift. As the guests arrived, the cakes were stacked up, and each time another one was added, fresh fruit, cream, honey, fruit syrup, or preserves was spread between the layers. A tall cake was a sign that the bride and her family were very popular. And when someone grabbed the pressed glass cake stand, and put the little pile of cakes up there, the bride immediately felt like a queen.

Apple butter-making revolves around a big cast iron pot simmering over a hardwood fire. The process lends itself to big group activity, which is what makes it perfect for Southern socializing. It happens in the fall, when apples ripen, which is also time for Thanksgiving, slaughtering hogs, smoking meat, sharing the harvest, canning produce, and a thousand other reasons to bring family and friends together. If nothing else, they want to visit because they know the coming winter weather means they might not see much of each other for a few months. There's often a chill in the air and a little fog clinging around the shoulders of the hills when the fire is kindled before dawn. As the sun appears with a promise to warm the day, wagons and trucks bring the neighbors and their baskets of apples. With children running and playing, and familiar voices calling greetings, people peel the red and yellow fruits, slice them, and add them to the big cast iron kettle simmering over a smoky wood fire. They keep feeding the fire and stirring the pot for hours until it's all done, the jars are sealed, and everybody goes home with apple butter for a whole winter's worth of biscuits. Folks still make apple butter throughout America, but the gathering, the good times, the shared work, and the handed-down memories, are all reasons that it remains a joyous part of life in the South.

There are plenty of regional and ethnic variations of apple butter, including some Northern versions that included the distinctive licorice-tasting spice anise. In general, recipes call for cider, which is apple juice made by slicing and simmering apples until tender, then putting them through a press, or simply letting them drip through a strainer. The juice is boiled again before canning. Cider is only available in the season in which it's made. In other words, if it's going to be used for apple butter, it has to be made within a few days of the apple butter-making. That's because apple juice will start turning to alcohol in about a week, even if it's kept cool. So if a cook ever started to make apple butter and found out the family's juice had turned to "hard cider," it couldn't be used. But they could still cook the apples in water and add one-fourth teaspoon of vinegar, instead of cider, and the apple butter-making could go on.

Audrey Stanfield Asling grew up learning to make apple butter on an Arkansas farm. But later, living in a suburban home where she couldn't have a big kettle on a wood fire, she invented a uniquely modern way to recreate that rich, old-time flavor in her apple butter. She cooked the apples in an iron pot, put them through a Foley Food Mill to remove the skins, and combined the pulp with other ingredients in the same iron pot. Then she put the pot on a charcoal grill for hours, with no lid on the pot, closing the grill's hood to hold the smoke in, adding a rich, smoky flavor to the apple butter. Oak, apple, cherry, or maple wood added to the taste. Audrey was said to cook the apple butter "until it was the color of a mahogany cabinet."

In Appalachia, a feeds a fire that will burn down to coals for cooking on the grill, using sheets of tin to adjust the flow of air. (Courtesy of Library of Congress)

Chapter 14

Home Is Wherever the Hearth Is

Inventors were trying to perfect kitchen stoves and ovens long before 1800, but the few that came on the market were big, heavy, expensive, and inefficient. Like a lot of things, stoves matured after the Civil War, when the foundries that had gobbled up America's iron, steel, tin, and brass to maintain a steady supply of weapons and equipment to the military, could turn their technology to the things that families needed. The factories were in the North, so stoves were manufactured in the North and sold to Northerners, and Northern coal mines were busy turning out coal to be burned in Northern stoves. In the South, with its boundless hardwood forests, the fireplaces, home heating stoves, and cooking stoves, all burned wood. Gradually, the market opened up, with stoves that had catchy names like the Hardwicks Wildwood, the Quaker Social, and the Mayflower. The popular Monitor, introduced in 1874, was advertised in sizes and configurations "to fit any kitchen," from sixteen to sixty-five dollars.

When people who'd been cooking in the fireplace got their first kitchen stove, they had to learn to cook all over again. The technology was brand new, some of the pots and pans were new, and yet there were still no thermostats for the ovens. Perhaps the biggest change of all, the heat on the stove top came into skillets and pots from the bottom, rather than the coming from the top, bottom, and sides in the fireplace. So cooks had to learn to keep food from burning on the bottom. Still, a wood-burning, cast iron kitchen stove was a back saver for cooks. Tending its little firebox with a latching door was a lot easier, not to mention cleaner and safer, than bending, kneeling, and reaching into a soot-blackened fireplace with sticks of firewood and heavy iron pots. The kitchen stove cooked more efficiently, gave the cook more precise control of the heat, and in warm weather, didn't put as much heat out into the house as a fireplace.

And yet, even as stoves became more efficient and easier to use, even as they became fueled with natural gas, then electricity, it was in the same era that the South still gave birth to barbecue. Among all the South's contributions to American culture, from Tennessee Williams, the steamboat, Elvis Presley, and bourbon, to the cotton gin, Baptist hymns, the drawl, and peanut butter, perhaps none stands taller than the art of the barbecue. Certainly, outdoor grilling is popular all over the country, but in the South, it's culinary religion. It's worthy of major investments of a family's time and money. It demands experimenting, learning, perfecting a repertoire of family favorites, and competing with a cook's own best successes, as well as with friends' finest creations. In the South, everybody does it, and one of the highest compliments we can pay is to say, "Hey, ya'll want to come over and grill out?"

Why is that the ultimate expression of our hospitality? Why do we love our barbecue so much? It's the culmination of a story that started in colonial times.

Every home had a fireplace built for cooking, usually with a broad raised hearth. Baked goods could bake there on the hearth in front of the fire, which was evidence of just how much heat the fire put out into the house. So cooking in the fireplace was a great winter activity. On those cold nights when icy winds found their way through every crack between the logs and around the doors, houses just never got warm, so the best place to be was by the fire. Beds sat high up off the floor to keep sleepers up out of the heavy, chilly air that settled along the floor. On the other hand, winter weather doesn't stick around very long in the South. Southern houses could get unbearably hot during the day, with the sun bearing down from a cloudless sky, and temperatures soaring so high in the afternoon that it never got cool at night. In the warm, steamy months, some folks liked sleeping on a pallet on the floor because it was cooler. That's just the way things were and had always been, and still, there was no sense in making it worse with an unbearable cooking fire in the fireplace. So in the hot and humid South, for up to nine months of the year, families cooked and ate outside.

Every house had a fire ring in the yard to boil the laundry water. There was hot water for washing, and sometimes both a warm and a cold tub for rinsing. Many families maintained a separate fire ring for cooking, and some went so far as to build elaborate masonry fire pits. In time, those gave rise to the barbecue pit. Like everything else in America, folks kept finding ways to make it a little better. The masonry pits grew chimneys and iron grills, which grew bigger, so there was space for both high heat and warming, and the cooks got better at using their fire circles, or barbecue pits, or whatever they had, to grill, fry, roast, and bake more foods.

Mariam Colt, the vegetarian pioneer wife who was so happy to move from a New York house with a kitchen to a one-room sod house on the Kansas prairie, wrote in her diary that her kitchen's roof was "the blue dome of heaven." Most people today wouldn't think it was all that romantic, trying to fix a tasty, nourishing meal out there in the rain, dust, and never-ending wind. Women did most of the cooking, and they worked around fires, indoors and out, all day, all year. There were fires in the fireplace and fires in the cook stove, if they had one. There were fires under the wash pot, and hotter fires for scalding the hair and feathers off of slaughtered animals. The women's hands were roasted, and the bottoms of their work dresses were singed off. In fact, it wasn't uncommon for a pioneer woman to be badly burned when her dress caught fire. Still, in the August heat, an outdoor fire on the shady side of the house was better than cooking indoors.

Pots, pans, and utensils from the kitchen could also be used outdoors, but outdoor cooking also opened up some opportunities for innovation. With a Sears and Roebuck catalog, mother could make nest eggs. She'd soak a few catalog pages in water, break an egg on each one, twist it up into a ball, set it into the glowing coals at the edge of the fire, and three minutes later the egg was cooked. The same technique could be used with anything that would roast quickly inside the wet paper, like diced onion, squash, and peppers. That was adapted from the old Native American technique of putting small bits of food into a bed of almost any kind of green leaves, then mud, then plunging the bundle into the

A former slave cooks in a big fireplace with a variety of cast iron pots and pans. Extra handles hang on the chimney.

In 1900, a couple keeps warm beside the hearth in their one-room cabin. A pot of soup simmers in a cast iron pot, a cat snuggles at the woman's feet, and paper covers the walls to help insulate against the cold. (Courtesy of the Library of Congress)

embers. In fact, Native Americans also wove baskets just for this purpose, using them as the liner for a permanent clay cook pot or a one-use mud wrap.

In the absence of a grill, food was also cooked on hot stones and slabs of wood. Everybody loved the smoky taste of bread baked over an outdoor fire, instead of in an oven. A piece of chestnut or hickory bark could be used as a baking dish, with the dough spread out, and

the bark propped up beside the hot coals. They also made twist bread, wrapping the dough around a stick, which was poked into the ground and turned every few minutes as the side toward the fire browned. Meat was particularly good when cooked on slabs of cedar or juniper, which was the predecessor of the cedar planks for grilling that are sold in grocery stores today. Big cuts of meat, or an entire animal carcass could be roasted on an iron spit, and if the family didn't have an iron spit, a wooden one would do for roasting smaller game, like rabbits. They cooked their meat the same way chefs do today, as shown in an 1800 recipe that calls for a roast to be put over a hot fire so it cooked "quickly on the outside and less inside." Then the heat would be reduced, so the meat cooked slowly to the center, and "It should be basted and checked with a fork for doneness, rare being the healthiest and best tasting." The slave narratives include Ann Drake's description of the men in her family cooking a whole cow. "First, he dug a pit, and then that pit was covered with green poles, and then meat was laid over that fire. Then old Sam and old Levi had pitchforks and turned that meat over and over 'til it was nice and brown, then they put sauce on it."

And it's there, at the word "sauce," that the Southern grilling story takes a turn.

Pork, the preferred meat of the South since at least the early 1800s, cooks very well over a wood fire, but can become dry. Beef dries out more quickly. Poultry and wild game are prone to dry out very quickly in the flames. And dry meat is what led to the South's fascination with sauces.

Barbecue never would have reached its pervasive popularity without barbecue sauce, and barbecue sauce would never have appeared if British sailors of the 1700s hadn't made a poor attempt to pronounce an Asian word for fish sauce. As they mispronounced the word, it sounded like "ketchup." The Asian fish sauce didn't have any tomatoes in it, like our familiar tomato ketchup, because Asians thought tomatoes were poisonous. But when nobody in England seemed to be able to recreate the Asian sauce, they tried to all kinds of imitations, including many that had a tomato base. Those were pretty good.

Before ketchup, people generally topped their meat with gravy. Sometimes lots of gravy, depending on how overcooked and dry the meat was. So when ketchup was invented in England, it became enormously popular. Then the earliest American settlers made ketchup, and it can be credited with creating an American taste for tangy-sweet meat sauce with a tomato base. During the 19th century, recipes abounded for ketchups made with plums, peaches, cherries, oysters, wine, mussels, walnuts, mushrooms, and even celery. Some adhered to the traditional tomato base, while others had no tomatoes or tomato sauce in them, but instead had plenty of vinegar.

Barbecue sauce came about as a departure from ketchup, simply because cooking over fires, particularly outdoor fires, with their imprecise temperatures and unpredictable flare-ups, and with the meat exposed to flames, rather than being protected in a pot with a lid, could lead to dried-out food. Ketchup, in all its variations, was being used as a topping, and then people used it more and more for marinating and basting the meat as it cooked.

PORCH TALK

Pearl Moon Stanfield's mother died when she was just five years old, the youngest of nine children, with the oldest in their early teens. To keep the household functioning, the children took over all the chores, with each one responsible for getting specific jobs done. Pearl did all the laundry in a big iron kettle over a fire out in the yard. It was hard work, she says, but it had its benefits. If one of the other kids made her mad, she'd starch their underwear.

Some meat is marbled and edged with fat, which provides a certain amount of self-basting. But wild game in particular has virtually no fat, so it's easy for the cook to accidentally let it become dry, tough, and tasteless. Besides, keeping the meat moist by bathing it with sauces of various flavors gave the menu some excitement and variety. So repeatedly basting meat became part of the artistry of outdoor cooking. Ketchup wasn't actually the best thing for the job because it contained too much sugar, which burned quickly and made the meat too sweet. Most ketchups also didn't contain enough acid, which was needed to tenderize the meat and cut the fat.

PORCH TALK

Before thermometers became widely available, cooks used the touch method to check the temperature of their wood stove. If the hand could be left on the cooking surface for so many seconds, that told them the temperature. Checking the oven that way wasn't quite as risky as checking the top. If a bare hand could be kept in the oven to a full count of twenty, the oven was hot enough to bake a cake or slow roast meat. But if the cook could only stand to keep a hand in the oven to a count of five or six, the oven was too hot, well over 475 °F. It was safer, if not more accurate, to spread one-fourth of an inch of flour on the bottom of an inverted pan and leave it for five minutes. If the flour turned delicate brown, the oven was 250-300, and if it turned golden brown, the temperature was 350-400. But it had to be checked at three minutes, because if the flour had already turned dark brown, the oven was already up to 450 degrees.

Reflecting on those days in Arkansas, Pearl smiles and says a good cook "just knows" when the temperature is right.

Then Heinz, a Pennsylvania company that was marketing the first successful mass-produced ketchup, introduced commercial barbecue sauce to the world in 1871. It was modestly profitable, and like many commercial foods, the South was the last place it was distributed and Southerners were slow to embrace it. Southern cooks continued to experiment with their own sauces, mixing everything from water to animal fat to fruit and vegetable blends and vinegar, resulting in an ongoing, decades-long evolution of barbecue sauce that still goes on today. And that lead to the great, long-running, and continuing barbecue divide: tomato sauce versus vinegar sauce.

Voices and fists have been raised and insults hurled in defense of the two major divisions in the world of barbecue sauce. Both tomato-based and vinegar-based sauces are used for basting, as well as for topping and dipping meats. And there's no explanation for the regional biases for each, with vinegar sauces most popular along the East Coast, and tomato sauces reigning in most of the rest of the country. Both of them are messy, with vinegar sauces dripping onto shirt fronts and pants, and tomato sauces left sticking to fingers, napkins, and mustaches. Vinegar sauces, or Carolina sauces, are made with vinegar, black pepper, and hot pepper flakes. They have little or no sugar in them, and people like them because they're thin, so they soak into the meat, and their taste is "sharp," so it cuts through the tastes of meat and fat. Tomato sauces are generally rich with sweeteners and spices, and come in a variety of flavors, from very sweet to very hot and spicy. They often follow another thin basting sauce, and are applied in the last few minutes of cooking, so they cling to the meat with a cooked-on coating of rich flavor and texture, making them the preferred sauce for ribs.

Sauces are sweetened with everything from honey to cane sugar and maple sugar, and those sweet sauces have become especially popular in the North and in Texas. Even vinegar-sweet sauces have emerged. In Louisiana and across the Deep South, the spiciest, even downright hot sauces, are more popular, along with blends of peppers, as well as combinations of sweeteners and spices, known as sweet-hot sauces.

Some cooks turn their backs on sauces, and instead use a dry rub, literally rubbing the raw meat with their own favorite blend of spices, which usually includes a lot of black pepper. Over the fire, the mixture slowly blends with the meat's own juices, and that's why some folks believe that rubs produce the best results with fatter cuts of meat, like ribs. There are so many varieties of barbecue sauce, so many marinades, and so many rubbing, basting, smoking, grilling, and blackening techniques, anyone who likes outdoor cooking can find their favorite tastes. And that's what Southerners have been doing for well over a century. What began as survival cooking has become artistry.

A pan of golden rolls can be baked with white flour and almost any mixture of meal and grain, as long as it gets just the right leavening. (Courtesy of Tina Hargrove Ahern)

Chapter 15

Baking Day

Baking is not a science, but a delicate art. It requires patience, attention to detail, an understanding of how various ingredients work together, and most importantly, a lot of baking. One learns to bake by baking. The cook has to know which cookie sheets make the best cookies. What happened the last time they substituted white sugar for brown sugar. What browning looks like, and how fast it changes from "almost" to "uh oh."

There was a time when cooks made biscuits every day, from a simple mixture of flour, salt, baking powder, and grease or shortening. The best biscuits, sometimes called biscuits supreme, include a little sugar, plus cream of tartar, which makes them taller, lighter, and fluffier. Cut biscuits are cut out of a sheet of dough, while drop biscuits are a ball of dough "dropped" onto a cookie sheet. Cat head biscuits are big drop biscuits that rise to be, of course, as big as a cat's head. Folks love the peaks and valleys of their tender, brown crust, and besides being sliced like any other biscuit, they can also be dropped into simmering broth for creamy, sweet dumplings.

Even with all those daily biscuits, in most households there was also a baking day, maybe once a week, when most of the baking was done. There was so much preparation, and it made such a mess, it was just better to do a lot of it at one time. Then there was the matter of getting the wood stove to exactly the right temperature and keeping it there for hours while everything baked. It required a sizeable stack of wood beside the stove, cut and split to the right size to fit the stove.

Well-equipped kitchens of the late 1800s had a thermometer designed specifically to tell the temperature of their wood-burning stove's top or oven. Then, one of the best inventions to come along, beginning in about 1910, was the gas stove, which came with a built-in oven thermostat. Gas was initially used for street lights, so getting it piped into homes took years, and then it took a few more years for families to warm up to the concept, not to mention being able to afford a brand new gas stove. While all that was happening, city homes were being wired for electric lights, and electric stoves were being improved. Although many American homes, especially in the South, continued to cook with wood, the shift to gas and electric had taken over all across the country by 1940. With their thermostats and burner controls, cooks could use the right temperatures when following their recipes. When baking, they could know exactly when the oven reached the desired temperature, and they could time the baking more accurately. In the same era, measuring spoons and cups became more widely available, and more homes became able to afford them. Results became more predictable, which was an improvement that benefitted baking more than any other

In many homes, every day started with making biscuits. (Courtesy of Tina Hargrove Ahern)

type of cooking, because the tiniest variation can make a big difference in how baked goods turn out.

Everybody loves a loaf of fresh-from-the-oven bread they can slice and douse with butter. What gives risen bread its texture is leavening, an ingredient that produces a chemical reaction, releasing gas bubbles in a dough that's tough enough to hold the bubbles when the dough gets into the hot oven and starts to dry. From ancient times, Native Americans knew that corn was a leavening agent, and cornbread dough, when left in a warm place for a day or more, would rise. But the rest of the world didn't have corn in those days, so for centuries, people in other lands leavened bread with potash, a mixture of water and hardwood ashes, boiled, then filtered through a cloth. Potash, which is rich in potassium, was generally combined with an acid such as vinegar to get just the right amount of leavening. It worked, but some vinegar was strong, and some was weak, some potash was thick, and some thin, and there

A kitchen in transition. In about 1910, this woman cooks on her wood-burning stove, while on the table behind her, a two burner gas stove keeps a kettle warm. (Courtesy of the Library of Congress)

were no hard and fast rules about how much of each was needed. So those methods were pretty unpredictable, and early leavened bread was sometimes called quick bread. The cook had to get it in the oven quickly, before the leavening was lost.

Later, grated white potatoes, also called Irish potatoes, were commonly used as leavening. Potatoes have a particularly odd history, considering that they're packed with nutrients and easy to grow in a variety of environments. Like any root crop, the dirt in which they grow provides some insulation from temperature fluctuations and gives them a long growing season. So it makes sense that they would have spread around the world quickly and easily. Instead, they were grown in early South American civilizations, but didn't spread to North America with the same popularity of corn, peppers, and other foods. They were also cultivated in Spain, but were slow to spread to the rest of Europe. It wasn't until the 1800s that they become extremely popular in Europe, especially in Ireland, which led to the great potato famine of the 1840s. Perhaps as many as one million people starved in Ireland, and the suffering led to the great Irish immigration to America. Of course, the Irish brought with them their love for potatoes, not only to eat, but also to leaven baked goods.

Leavening is mentioned in the Bible and was used by the ancient Egyptians. But for centuries the process of producing gas bubbles to make the bread rise varied from one batch to another, and was poorly understood. In fact, like many scientific phenomena, it was regarded as magic, partly because it worked in making wine and beer the same way it worked in baking. It wasn't until the 1860s that Louis Pasteur identified the microorganisms in yeast, leading to commercial yeast late in the century, which led to more standardized results in the kitchen. Cooks could depend on yeast to leaven the same way every time.

But long before cooks could go to the store and buy a little paper-wrapped packet of yeast, ancient people customarily saved a little of their dough to start the leavening in the next batch of bread. And so it was that later American cooks set aside a handful of dough in a little wooden bowl, coated with flour, and covered with a towel, as a "starter" for the next batch. After all, they baked every week, if not every day. And even if they didn't understand that yeast feeds on sugars to release carbon dioxide, they knew they had to keep their starter cool until they were ready to use it. A bit of the starter was broken off and used for each batch of biscuits, and the remaining starter was guarded like a treasure. Large-scale baking required some planning ahead. The starter was added to flour and kneaded with warm water, then left near the warm stove, where it rose, and by the next morning it provided enough leavening for two or three bushels of flour. If a household ran out of starter, or if the starter froze or dried out and died, the cook would have to get a new starter, a simple ball of dough, or later, a bit of yeast, from a neighbor, which of course provided a good opportunity for a nice visit over a cup of coffee.

Traditionally, the ideal bread, the best fine-textured loaf bread with a tender crust, is made with some combination of wheat flour with baking powder, baking soda, and yeast. Baking powder and baking soda are combinations of chemicals that can be used in place of yeast, give the same kind of dependable results, and are much easier to store and use. If a cook is making a soft, chewy cookie, such as a chocolate chip cookie, they would use baking soda, which will allow the cookie to spread. If they're making rolled and cut cookies, such as sugar cookies or gingerbread men, they'd use baking powder. Baking powder makes cookies rise, but doesn't make them spread very much.

Anything a cook could need for baking was on the market in the 1800s, but just because something is being sold in some stores doesn't mean the folks back in the hills can get it. In the old South, with fewer stores than in other parts of the country, and fewer rails with fewer trains bringing fewer products to the stores, products often weren't as fresh as they should be. Cooks learned to carefully ration their baking soda and baking powder so they didn't run out, and still, it could happen. So if the cook ran out of the right type of leavening agent, it was better to use a substitute than to go without. If they ran out of baking powder, they can make their own by combining two parts cream of tartar to one part baking soda and one part cornstarch. To substitute baking powder for baking soda, they'd use one teaspoon of baking powder for every one cup of flour.

All of that is why some heirloom baking recipes today still call for a spoon or two of vinegar. Such a recipe is probably an old one that was originally made without baking powder or soda or yeast. Later, even after baking powder and baking soda became readily available, cooks often continued to hand down recipes that retained all the old ingredients along with the new, and that's why some recipes today say to use both vinegar and baking powder, when it's really not necessary; vinegar only enhances the baking powder's natural action. On the other hand, there's a very good reason why vinegar appears in the common recipe for never fail pie crust. It limits the production of gluten in the dough, and that creates a crust that's tender and flaky, instead of having the texture of bread.

The problems of getting and keeping store-bought leavening agents led many cooks to sourdough bread. Chemically, sourdough is different from common wheat bread because it doesn't need baker's yeast, baking powder, or baking soda. The flour provides the only leavening. Like many bread recipes, two-thirds of the flour went into mixing the dough, with the last third added as the dough is kneaded. A good cook knows when it reaches the "right" consistency, and then it's left to rise overnight, divided into loaves, and left to rise again before baking. It became very popular in the American West, where, like the South, it was often hard to find proper baking ingredients. Sourdough became so popular during the California gold rush that a common nickname for a miner was "sourdough." Many a crusty miner wore a cloth bag around his neck containing a bit of sourdough starter, with his body keeping it at just the right temperature, year around, so that with a little salt, flour, and water, he could bake some bread.

A cook can make a new sourdough starter

PORCH TALK

Flour was so precious, even when it went bad, or "indifferent," people found a way to use it. Cookbooks said if the flour wouldn't make good "light bread," sometimes it would still make good biscuits. The recipe called for a spoonful of salt to a quart of flour, a teacup of milk, lard the size of an egg, and just enough water to make a stiff dough. Then the dough had to be beaten for thirty minutes before cutting the biscuits. That's a lot of work for a batch of biscuits, but cooks would do anything to keep from throwing flour out. Some cooks said it was much the same with people; the right ingredients and a little work can save even the worst of us.

from a simple mixture of flour and water that's left overnight to ferment. Then a little more flour and water are added, and it's left to sit again. That process is repeated until the starter is bubbly and sour-smelling, which takes about five days, if everything goes right and the cook keeps the right ratios of starter culture, water, flour, and warmth. The longer it ferments, the bigger the bubbles, or holes, and the lighter the bread. Sourdough bread has a slightly sour taste that many people prefer and is now known to be easier to digest than yeast bread. Cooks like it too, as long as they have some starter on hand and don't have to go back to the beginning and repeat that five-day process.

Like everything else in the rural diet, the fat used in baking was often dictated by what was available. Butter provided the best flavor, but in the crusts of certain pies, bacon grease was the only choice. Traditionally, Southern cooks never combined butter and lard, but many cooks today believe that combination gives the best result. Shortening, like Crisco, which is all vegetable fat, became available about 1912. It can be used to replace most other fats, which makes it more convenient than saving different kinds of grease in various containers. It also has no flavor, so it imparts no flavor to the food. But shortening certainly has its limitations. First of all, the flavor of bacon grease is a pretty good reason to use bacon grease. And some of the best pie makers say their crusts suffer if they use shortening, so they refuse to use it.

To understand the tradition of baking in the old South requires an understanding of how rare and precious white flour was. Wheat has been cultivated, milled, and used in baking for centuries, and has always required a huge investment of labor. After planting and harvesting, there was still threshing to knock the tiny kernels loose from their hulls, called chaff. Then there was winnowing to separate the chaff, and then sifting. Ancient farmers beat wheat stalks on stones, then later used flails. Threshing machines did that work after 1800, and the combine, a horse-drawn machine that mowed and threshed the wheat in one giant, clanging operation, came on the scene just before the Civil War, though its manufacture was delayed by the demands of manufacturing armaments. Even later, when America's factories turned back to making farm machinery, the process of growing, cutting, and threshing enough wheat to make the hundreds of pounds of flour that a family would need in a year was beyond the reach of most farmers. People with rocky little farms east of the Mississippi River didn't have enough land to grow wheat, and they surely couldn't afford a combine.

Grinding wheat into a fine powder was a technically precise process, compared to the ease with which corn could be taken to the local mill for grinding, or even ground at home with a grinding stone. Flour had to be ground much finer than cornmeal, and the best milling was done by smooth steel rollers. Flour was milled, rather than ground, as it was pressed between the rollers, and that all became even more complex as new varieties of wheat and flour were introduced. There were soft, medium, and hard strains of wheat. White flour was made from only the endosperm, the white part of the kernel, which required that the bran and germ were removed in separate steps. After milling, the flour was bleached to make it white. Whole wheat flour, made from grinding the whole-wheat kernel, was easier to produce, but spoiled quickly. It was all suited to huge scale commercial production, and a technical impossibility to a farm family.

During the first half of the nineteenth

century, American wheat was being grown in horizon-wide fields, from Nebraska, north into Canada, and east to the Great Lakes, and it all was shipped east for milling. The first big mills appeared in Minneapolis in the mid-1850s. When horse-drawn threshing machines appeared in the Northern fields, they required big crews of men and horses, and all of that was owned and operated by harvesting companies. As wheat production increased, new mills were built, stretching South by 1870 to St. Louis, which boasted twenty-seven mills with the finest steel rollers. Also in the 1870s, Mennonite farmers introduced winter wheat to America. It was planted in the fall, and overwintered to be harvested in early summer. So within a few years, the nation was generating two wheat harvests, one in the North, and one extending South all the way into Texas and west into Colorado. But still, it all pointed back to mills in the North and East.

It was gigantic. Wheat brokers and millers joined in exchange clubs that merged with chambers of commerce to wield amazing power. Investors found that it was a lot more profitable to send wheat and flour down the Mississippi and out through the Great Lakes, exporting it to the ports of the world, than to shuttle it to California and the American South by multiple trains and wagons. For example, when wheat was shipped from a field in eastern Colorado to St. Louis, where it was milled, then packed, and shipped south to a little store in a little town in the middle of Georgia, of course it was going to be very expensive. So nearly all of the wheat flour consumed in America went to the bustling Great Lakes and eastern cities, simply because they were closer to mills and railroads. White flour and white bread continued to be the staple of city wage earners, and out of reach for a lot of common folks.

But the 1870s is also when Charles Alfred Pillsbury started meeting with engineers to secretly plan the world's biggest and most advanced mill. When his technological marvel, Pillsbury Mill A, opened in Minneapolis in 1878, it could handle ten times the volume of other mills of the time, and yet was operating at only about ten percent capacity. Clearly, Pillsbury was banking on the future of white flour in America. As wheat production rose by 500 percent during the 1880s, so did distribution to the heart of the nation.

Meanwhile, smaller milling machines, including some about the size of a desk,

PORCH TALK

Some people say biscuits were invented so we'd have a way to eat red-eye gravy, which is thin, greasy, salty, and ranges in color from coal black to blood red. It's been portrayed in popular culture as a cowboy favorite in the American West, and indeed, its simplicity makes it perfect for campfire cooking. But it has long flourished in the South simply because it's so good with biscuits, and Southerners eat lots of biscuits. It begins with frying some ham or salt pork in a skillet. After the meat is removed, the grease is spooned out, and enough coffee poured in to cover the pan. As the coffee boils, it loosens the meat drippings that were stuck to the pan. Then salt is added, and some of the grease is added back in, equal to the coffee. Like most gravies, it needs constant stirring. Some cooks add sugar, and black or red pepper.

With sugar and milk added, it thickens and becomes sawmill gravy. That's generally the preferred version for topping meat and potatoes. And anybody who's eaten it understands that it can provide the perfect analogy for a front porch poet, as in, "The love around that breakfast table was as thick as sawmill gravy."

with genuine steel rollers, were designed, manufactured, and installed all over the country in local mills and feed stores. Gradually, the availability of more wheat mills, plus improved rails and roads, meant more farmers could raise wheat and corn for their families, and get both milled locally. By the end of the century, white flour, white bread, flakey pie crusts, and golden biscuits were available to everyone. In 1890, some ninety percent of Americans baked their own white bread. Factory-baked, sliced bread wasn't even available until 1930, and even later in the rural South.

So once again, it was the South's deprivation, coupled with the resilience of its people that fueled their triumph. All of that Midwestern history with white flour and white bread, over all those years, meant a great deal to the nation. But in the South, it meant that people had spent those years without white flour and white bread making other kinds of baked goods. And that meant the South was, and would continue to be, the home of a more diverse menu of baked goods than any other part of the country.

PORCH TALK

Pearl Moon Stanfield took it for granted that every morning started with making biscuits in the wood stove's oven, and the rest of the day's menu descended from that. After a breakfast of biscuits, the men would go to work, and the children would go to school, with a lunch of something—a slice of ham, a fried egg, or maybe just some jam—on a biscuit wrapped in newspaper. It gave them a laugh when they unwrapped their lunch at noontime, because they could read the day's news on the bottom of the biscuit.

Traditional cornbread was as simple as blending corn meal, flour, eggs, and baking powder. Then, when white flour became common, the addition of a little white flour made lighter, fluffier cornbread. White flour also gave cooks more opportunities to mix more ingredients into their bread, which improved their recipes for pumpkin bread, apple nut bread, and persimmon bread. So the availability of white flour didn't mean cooks suddenly switched to it. Rather, white flour became part of their repertoire as they went on making vegetable and fruit bread, quick breads, and fried breads, often flavored with onions or sweeteners.

The varieties of breads and creative baking techniques are astonishing. In Texas, the Simpson's son, J. R., would stop in at the hardware store on his way home from work and buy some bran. It was available at the food store, but was a lot cheaper at the hardware store. On any day they might have had rice, wheat, barley, or even oat bran, and he'd buy whatever was available and fresh. He'd take it home and throw it into a greased cast iron skillet with a little salt and milk, and bake some bran bread. Simple as that. "Johnny cakes" was a name that came to be applied to various small breads, but originally, Johnny cakes were rice flour biscuits that were basted with milk while baking before an open fire. Georgia sunlight bread, an all-day recipe that dates to before the Revolutionary War, started before 7:00 a.m. with a cup of scalded milk. A spoonful of flour, one of cornmeal, and a little water were added before setting the mixture in the warm morning sun. The trick was to stir it frequently, but as one recipe specifies, "when you see bubbles, don't stir no more." That usually happened by 9:00 a.m., then it was left to rise in the sun until about 2:00 p.m., when that little bit of starter became the leavening

This grain elevator was the heart of the Lillie Mill flour milling company, founded 1869 in Franklin, Tennessee. Such mills revolutionized Southern baking by making white flour more available.

for a whole loaf. Flour, salt, sugar, and lard were added, then the dough was kneaded and left in the sun to rise again before baking.

Somebody could always find a use for leftover baked goods. Extra pie crust dough just needed a little sugar and cinnamon to become a treat for the children. There was also ham and egg pie. And Cush, which is a fried mixture of bacon drippings and crumbled leftover biscuits and cornbread. Cold biscuits could be brought to life when they were split, put in a skillet, and covered with canned tomatoes and cream gravy.

Soda bread is a perfect example of the adaptability of Southern cooks and their recipes. It probably originated in England, and became known as an Irish favorite by the middle 19th century. It's made with baking soda and little or no baking powder, creating a heavy, round, pull-apart or slicing loaf, a perfect, chewy compliment to soups and stews. Plus, it was easier and quicker than yeast breads, which generally require kneading and rising twice. It was a favorite when it was made with whole wheat flour, and after white flour became widely available, cooks made it with a mixture of white and whole wheat flours. The recipe calls for buttermilk or sour milk. It could be made with almost any kind of fat, from butter to bacon grease. There's twice as much sugar as salt. With floured fingers the cook formed it into a round loaf, then sliced the top in a cross, all the way around the edges, which let it rise while it was baking without cracking the crust. Some people like a hard, crunchy crust on their soda bread, but if the fresh loaf is taken out of the oven and allowed to cool in a towel, the crust holds the moisture in, and that makes the crust more tender. Audrey Stanfield Asling checked her soda bread for doneness by taking it out of the oven and tapping it on the bottom. If it sounded hollow, it was done.

Chapter 16

The Sweets

Cooks have been known to experiment endlessly with desserts. Only by some experiment long ago could someone have figured out that they could make grape pie only if they squeezed the pulp out of the skins, cooked the pulp, then added the skins back in, and cooked it all again. In the kitchen, creativity flows like electricity when thoughts turn to surprising sweets that will not only satisfy the family's sweet tooth, but also get the loved ones talking, joking, sharing, and remembering. Spending the time and energy to make a special dessert is one of the most loving things a cook could do, because it requires at least an hour of attention, along with a knowledge of ingredients and a sense about when and how to do every step.

People everywhere love chocolate, and that's especially true in the Northern states, with their close ties to their European roots. There, people put a lot of their dessert-making energy into things made with chocolate, including chocolate cookies. They tend to follow ethnic and national origins for their sweets, creating German, Danish and Swedish pastries, along with exotic cakes with imported ingredients, icing between layers, toppings, blended creams, and fancy, decorative icing on top. But in the South, sweets took a different direction. There was no chocolate during the Civil War, and little of it for years afterwards. Southern desserts were based on fruit, depending on what was in season or what was preserved in the pantry and the cellar. And Southerners had little white flour until well after the war, so the South became home to pies, cobblers, and other treats that were relatively simple, compared to some of the lush sweets that were being cooked up North.

Cooks who do a lot of baking understand that most cakes are simply a sweeter, lighter version of a quick bread. The regional difference is that Northern breads tended to be more savory, flavored with spices, while Southern breads were made from a wide variety of vegetables and fruits. There are both breads and cakes of blueberry, carrot, and even watermelon, because the basic ingredients are the same. The same cooked pumpkin can be used in dough for bread and in batter for cake.

So Southern cooks make very fine cakes, but Southerners have always leaned toward pies. They're generally made with fruit, which is abundant in the South, and Southerners know how to preserve their fruit. Dried apples can make a pie as well as fresh apples. Cakes need up to five eggs, and some old cake recipes called for twenty eggs. Some were based on the weight of the eggs, calling for "half the egg weight in flour, a quarter of the egg weight in sugar," and so on. Then there's that pesky matter of white flour. Cakes need a lot of white flour, while pies need only a little, and can be made with none, using nut meal instead. Another factor that limited the popularity of cakes in the South was the wood-burning stove. It was used far longer in the South than in other parts of the country because wood was basically free, and because the South was slower to get natural gas and electricity. An oven in a wood-burning stove may have heated unevenly, and it was really hard to maintain a steady heat. A cake required a lot of attention as the cook added wood and adjusted the damper to get just the right amount of fire to the oven, and the actual temperature in the oven could cycle up and down as the wood burned. If a cake's leavening agents don't get the right heat at the right time, the cake won't rise properly. And if there's too much or too little heat, a cake will end up doughy on the inside and tough on the outside. But pies are far more forgiving. When the crust is done, the pie's probably done.

Once a cook mastered the art of the pie crust, she could make almost any kind of pie, provided she had enough sugar. Cherries thrive in cooler climates, so cherry pie is more of a Northern favorite. But peaches do quite well in the South, and that's why peach pie became an icon of the Southern table. There were also blueberry, gooseberry, and blackberry pies, and the berries were free out in the woods. There was potato pie, sweet potato pie, sugar pie, and molasses pie, which could be made as simply as combining eggs, molasses, and butter, and pouring it into a crust. The tart taste of lemon pie is popular, but lemons are an imported luxury, and if they weren't available, Southern chefs could make an old familiar vinegar pie using the same recipe, but with vinegar instead of lemon juice.

It's no surprise that in a region that loves fried foods, fried pies became popular. A crust was rolled out, then cut into six-inch circles. The filling was added, then the crust folded over and pinched along the curved edge to create a puffy half-moon shape before the individual pies were slipped into bubbling oil to fry. There's a Northern version, the Jewish blintzes, and cheese fillings were among the best-loved. In the South, there were sweet potato and mincemeat fillings, which were usually served as a dinner entrée. But the most popular, especially for breakfast, were fruit fillings, such as those made with dried apples or peaches, which were boiled to reconstitute them, then heated with sugar and flour. Recipes specified that the amount of sugar depended on how sweet the dried fruit was, which could mean a lot of trial and error for a cook to get the sweetness just right. And even if there was no other filling, a pretty good fried pie could be made with jam.

White sugar is an expensive store-bought item, made from sugar cane or sugar beets in far-away factories. It's one thing that simply can't be made at home. Brown sugar is best in some dishes, but having both white and brown sugar in the pantry was quite a luxury in the old South. So when the family had sugar on hand, especially enough white sugar to make a cake or cobbler, it was a tangible, delicious sign of good times. But even without white sugar, folks found a way to get their sweets. Honey has always been free, even for our earliest ancestors, who braved bees to get a finger full of sweetness. Rural families knew how to locate a bee tree in the wood. All they had to do was watch and listen, and the bees would lead them to the hive. A little fire kindled at the base of the tree, with some green branches laid on to create lots of smoke, would calm the bees long enough to reach in with a stick, spoon, or knife, and cut out chunks of honey comb, which were

Myrtle Branson Simpson displays her pineapple upside down cake. (Courtesy of Tanya Touchstone)

dropped into a bucket. Back at the house, the honey was treated like gold, stored in a crock or glass jar, used in cooking, and served at the table in a special lidded bowl.

Another favorite sweetener was molasses, and once a person developed a taste for it, they were likely to be a lifelong devotee. The Moon family in Arkansas grew sugar cane and took it to nearby Hobtown for processing. The stalks were put into a press, which was turned by a mule, or later by a gasoline engine. The green juice of the cane was filtered as it flowed out into a long pan that was divided into sections. They say it was nasty green stuff at first, but the taste got better as the juice was slowly boiled over a carefully-controlled fire, and moved with wooden paddles from one section of the pan to the next, changing color to progressively darker brown. Gradually, the water boiled out of the juice, leaving the sugar more and more concentrated in the remaining syrup. The people cooking the juice took out some first molasses, which is thinner and lighter in color, and favored by some folks for pancakes. Second molasses was most common. And finally, the cooking could continue, eventually producing blackstrap molasses, with its strong taste and high mineral content. Molasses was sweet, yet bitter, and was a Southern favorite on pancakes and biscuits. It was called for in many recipes, and if a cook was out of brown sugar, she could make a perfect substitute by adding a little molasses to white sugar.

Jesse Farrow Pate starts the molasses-making process by putting cane through a press in Peytonsville, Williamson County, TN. (Courtesy of Debbie Smartt)

Folks loved suet pudding, which may be the easiest dessert of all. It's a boiled mixture of suet, sugar, flour, and salt. Suet is a fat that melts slower than butter or lard, and cooks discovered that it created air bubbles as it melted, which made some dishes, like simple pudding, lighter. All kinds of fruit can be added to suet pudding.

From ancient times, cooks have baked leftover dough into little hard cakes, but it was only in the last 200 years or so that they've been sweetened and called cookies. They were first offered in an American cookbook in 1796, and it listed only two varieties. Today, cookies owe their popularity in large part to the fact that there are so many colorfully-packaged, heavily-advertised brands in the stores. But home-made cookies take a lot of time and work, so in that respect, it's one of the greatest gifts a cook can give the family. Scottish immigrants brought their favorite, oat cakes, to America, and there were other contributions, including British shortbreads, Swedish sand cakes, and German lebkuchen.

Those cookies with ethnic and national origins, just like ethnic pastries, have traditionally been decorated with all sorts of icing, fruit, candy, and other toppings. But when a Southern cook like Blanche Davis, of Roane County, TN, made cookies, they were simple and sweet, like her tea cakes, which some people would call sugar cookies. She followed the same recipe her mother, and probably her mother, used. Her cookies were the size of a Moon Pie, lightly browned around the edges, and Blanche never added decorations or sugar on top, because they were sweet enough already. Her sons would eat them three or four at a time with a glass of milk, and even after the boys were grown up and came to visit with their families, Blanche always had a Tupperware container of tea cakes waiting.

Cookies have never been as popular as other sweets in the South, and there are several intertwining reasons for that. Northern cooks often leavened their cookies with powdered ammonia, another store-bought item that was rare in the South. It was a quick leavening agent that didn't start to rise until it went into the oven, and it helped the cookies turn out crisp, but still tender. Cookies also generally require white flour, and Southern cooks got a late start with flour. Perhaps more important, as with cakes, it was really hard to get cookies to turn out right, not burnt and not raw, in a wood-burning stove. So when it really came down to a choice, Southern cooks would rather bake something that contains fruit, like a pie or a cake. If they're going to make a dessert that's held in the fingers, it's likely to be bar cookies, with dough that's spread out in a pan, baked, and cut into pieces. Bar cookies can be made in endless varieties, including fruity ones like blackberry and apple nut.

The South's landmark contribution to the world of desserts may be peanut brittle. Historically, nuts of all kinds were viewed primarily as food, and not as snack items, like they are today. People really worked at gathering, sorting, shelling, and storing nuts, as various ones matured and fell from trees over a period of several months, from late

PORCH TALK

Hand-written in a North Carolina cookbook, describing pies with and without top crust, or with a lattice top crust: "There are three kinds of pies: Kivered pie, Unkivered pie, and Barred. Fruit pies are Kivered or Barred. Winter pies are Unkivered."

summer to late fall. They were free, and the trees didn't have to be tended like other crops. Nuts were chopped for breads and cakes, as well as ground into meal, to be used in place of flour or mixed with other grains. But just as sweet treats have always been a way for people to celebrate life, making treasured nuts into nut brittle is a sort of declaration of dietary independence, a way of saying, "We're livin' it up now."

There's an even greater perspective on this sweet treat, and it's related to the historic work of scientist and inventor George Washington Carver. Cotton was such a profitable cash crop in the South, farmers grew it year after year on the same land, in some places for 100 years. Any such repeated planting means the same plant is taking the same nutrients from the earth every year, and it steadily depletes the soil unless those nutrients are replenished. In much of the Deep South, cotton left a black gumbo soil that grew harder to plow, and each year provided a little less food for the cotton plants. Carver searched for alternative crops that would not only grow well in the South, but also restore the nutrients that years of cotton production had stripped away. That led to his most notable work, the improvement of the peanut, along

Nothing says "love" quite like a hot apple pie, fresh from the oven. Southerners have historically preferred pies to cakes for several reasons, including the fact that fruit grows so well in the South.

with the invention of multiple uses for peanuts and their oil. There, in the lowly peanut, he saw a multi-purpose food source that could be cultivated and harvested like any other crop, and was hardy and adaptable, with a more predictable, dependable yield than tree nuts, which can vary greatly, depending on weather and rainfall. Carver found that peanuts would flourish in depleted Southern soil, and like all legumes, they restored vital nitrogen to the earth. That understanding led to rotating peanuts with other crops, with greater year-around success. So, peanuts are a Southern scientific, cultural, and agricultural marvel, and of course Southern cooks made them a culinary marvel in all kinds of foods, including desserts

Before peanuts became peanut brittle, some cooks were already making sugar candy and brown sugar candy, and those recipes are essentially the same as brittle. The ingredients are simple, but cooking such a sugary mixture without burning it is an art. The trick to sugar candy, like most candy, is in the careful application of heat for just the right amount of time, with plenty of stirring. Southern cooks had also been treating their families to pralines, a French import that was a little easier to cook, and therefore spread throughout the South from New Orleans in the 1700s. A praline is round and soft, like a thick, chewy cookie, and may include walnuts or almonds. Since the American South is the premier environment for pecan trees, pecans became the popular choice. The candy in a praline is a blend of sugar, butter, cream or buttermilk, and a little cream of tartar, with some recipes calling for corn syrup. According to popular legend, brittle was born in the 1890s when a woman was making peanut pralines and accidentally omitted the cream of tartar.

True story or not, planned or not, the result was a cookie sheet full of flat, hard candy, and the only way to serve it was to break it into irregular, jagged pieces, producing some as big as cookies, and some as small as a bite. And that was birth of peanut brittle, which endures today as a Southern favorite.

In the fall, fresh fruit that hadn't been eaten, cooked into pies, or canned, was made into jelly, jam, and other spreads. Fruit jelly is made from juice that's been strained, so it's clear. Its natural pectin reacts when cooked with sugar to make it thicken. Jam includes tiny bits of fruit, and is cooked a shorter time. Preserves have fairly large chunks of fruit suspended in jelly, and a conserve is made from dried fruit that's suspended in a thick syrup, not jelly. A fruit honey is a thin mixture, and may be opaque, or translucent, like jelly. Audrey Stanfield Asling's Pear Honey recipe calls for eight cups of chopped pears, along with two cups of pineapple. The pineapple was included more for its acid than for the flavor it contributed. So in older times, when pineapple wasn't so easy to find in grocery store cans, cooks could substitute oranges, lemons, or even vinegar to provide the needed acid.

Part of the magic of sweets and desserts was that they've always been an unspoken celebration of the abundance of life. The time busy people devoted to making sweets was a luxury. Using hard-to-get, store-bought ingredients like white sugar was a luxury. And the joy of eating something frivolous was luxurious indeed. Every loving cook knows that sometimes folks who know hard work and hardship just need a dessert on the table to bring smiles to the faces of children and grown-ups alike.

A farmer walks up the lane at sunset, dry leaves crunching underfoot, a meal on the stove, and the promise of spring in the air.

Chapter 17

Southern Time

There's something about good, clean dirt. Southerners can often be seen staring at it. People will step outside a restaurant and stop to look around the shrubs, peering past the blooming petunias at the dirt they're growing in. Not looking for anything in particular. Just enjoying familiar somethings that other people might not notice. They can be seen on the porch with a cup of coffee in the morning, studying bare spots in the corners of their own yard the same way. While at a rural gas station waiting for the tank to fill up, they'll gaze across a fallow field as if someone's waiting for them to intuit what was recently harvested or announce what's going to be planted next season. They talk about red dirt, black dirt, dusty ol' brown dirt, sandy loam, rocky soil, gumbo that can't be cut with an axe, and clay that sticks to the tires. They wiggle a finger into a flower pot to see if it needs to be watered. Southerners just seem to carry an innate understanding that the soil below their feet gives and sustains life. Even if they don't say the Earth is their home, they've known it both literally and figuratively from birth.

They understood the undulating, rhythmic dance of land, water, weather, plants, people, and animals. It rarely snows in the South, and when it does, it melts the next day. Still, the winters are long and cloudy, dark and cold, looking and feeling like a time to hibernate. But in truth, winter is the time for fixing and mending, splitting firewood, and hunting one more young buck deer or tom turkey. Time for replacing axe handles, sharpening knives, and cooking the delicious foods that were canned, pickled, smoked, cured, and stored in cellars and spring houses the previous fall. There might even be a few hearty collard greens making it through the winter in a wind-sheltered corner of the garden, and those need to be picked and eaten. It's a perfect time to try new recipes or bring the old ones back around. And in winter, there's always somebody around to sample a loaf of pumpkin bread fresh from the oven. Winters have always been perfect for holding onto faith that the dark chill would sooner or later give way to the light of spring. For sitting by a warm fire with a pencil and paper, planning what would be planted in the spring, checking which seeds are on hand, and ordering new seeds from a catalog. It's always been the time when the bare trees twist and creak in the wind, giving views of distant hills, hollows, and houses that can't be seen in the green and leafy months. It's the time when deer teach their new fawns how to hide in the brown grass and leaves. And no matter what the weather, livestock have to be fed, stalls mucked out, cows milked, and chickens kept warm. Everybody's vigilant, because hungry predators can't find much prey in the woods, and they come closer to the house looking for an easy meal. Then it's time to repeat that old story about the February night when grandpa was sick, so grandma went out to lock up the barn, and how a cougar walked through the yard just as baby brother shuffled out onto the porch, and grandma had to chase the big cat away, rattling a milk pail all the way down the lane.

Then winter slips away and spring comes to tease. It's here, then it's gone, a balmy day followed by black storms that rip at the trees, tornadoes that tear at roofs, and cold snaps that seem to snarl and say, "It's not spring, yet." February, March, and April have always been time to get ready for warmer weather. Gardens had to be cleaned up, old leaves and vines thrown away, and fences fixed to keep the deer out and the livestock in.

Somewhere along there, the dirt had to be turned over and plowed in rows, and the cool weather crops had to be planted. People watched the clouds, talked to their neighbors, took their best guess, then prayed that the weather would cooperate. Collards, spinach, onions, and cabbage could be sowed. Tomatoes and peppers might be started in little pots in a South-facing room of the house or barn, where they'd get the best light and be protected from late cold snaps. Springtime warmth could be a long time coming, but it always came, and with it, longer days in the sun, planting, then hoeing the weeds, which always seemed to arrive earlier and survive better than the vegetables. The births of calves, piglets, ducklings, and chicks had to be attended, and the new lives made safe and warm.

Along about the middle of April it was time to reach into the familiar soil and check the temperature. If it had warmed sufficiently, it was time to plant lettuce. A couple of weeks later, the tomato and pepper seedlings could be set out. Then a couple of weeks later there was more excitement when corn, beans, squash, watermelon, cantaloupe, and okra seeds went into the ground. That was about the same time the first tender young greens could be harvested. Then suddenly the sun was rising higher and staying longer, and there was even more to do. The hoeing continued. The cold weather crops could have a second planting. Livestock was moved to different pastures. Hogs were turned out to find their own food among the roots, bits of fruit, and last fall's leaf-covered acorns in the woods. The beans and squash were ready. There was some kind of produce to pick every day. Late summer was brutally hot, with humid days in the broiling sun, and nights that never cooled, and the exhausted plants withered. But those days soon passed, and the fall garden had to be planted in August, returning to the plants that were happy to ripen in cool weather. With a little luck, a late freeze, and enough rain, there could be something to pick until about the middle of December.

And all that bounty had to be preserved. It was hard work making sure nothing spoiled. Peaches ripened, then pears. Pumpkins were ready just before the first freeze, and it was time to gather the last of the apples and start canning and making pies. There were also still green tomatoes on the vine that had to be harvested, and just before the first frost, there was a scurry to harvest the last of the other vegetables. If the tomatoes were kept in a cool, dark place, like on a tray under the bed, they'd ripen slowly over the course of three or four months. They were never as tasty as tomatoes that ripened on the vine, but still, there was a special kind of fun to eating red tomatoes in winter. On the other hand, most green tomatoes didn't last long enough to ripen because cooks had recipes for them. They could be baked in a pie, which some folks say tastes just like apple pie. But everybody loved the storied, beloved, iconic, hard-to-resist and easy to prepare, fried green tomatoes. The best tomatoes for frying are just ready to start turning color, when they have a good tart flavor, not yet too sweet. They're sliced one-fourth-inch thick, then some cooks like to dip them in milk, but they're naturally juicy, so some cooks skip that step. A little salt and pepper, a dredging in white corn meal, and the slices are dropped into hot bacon grease. Fried green tomatoes are generally considered a side dish, but some folks are happy to make them a sandwich or an entrée.

The turning of the seasons, with the use of hand-me-down skillets and tools, has a subtle way of reconnecting us to our ancestors. The more we know about them, the more amazing it seems that they accomplished anything, because the basic business of daily living used to take so much time and work. Before they could eat an egg, they had to raise the chickens and trudge through the rain to the henhouse, where they'd shoo the hens off the nest, just to bring in the eggs. To enjoy sautéed mushrooms, they had to gather them in the woods, and they had to make the wine in which to sauté them. To can green beans, they had to get a fire in the stove hot enough to boil the water to sterilize the jars. Just to get dressed, they had to make their own lye soap and do the laundry in big iron pots over wood fires. Still, our forefathers and foremothers found the time and energy to manage farms, start businesses, write the Constitution, and invent the cotton gin, zippers, tin cans, and banana pudding.

Of course, the South isn't all rife with pastoral scenes of rural families patiently tending their bountiful gardens and cooking the harvest preserved in the root cellar. Southern towns, large and small, which came back to life during Reconstruction, became some of the nation's most dynamic centers for business, technology, education, and trade. The South was reborn in the arts, business, science, sports, business, and more.

Still, it's funny that no matter how big and sophisticated the biggest Southern cities grew, they never lost their unique charm, which still flourishes today and doesn't exist anywhere else. Peggy Schugar Cadenhead grew up in Fort Payne, Alabama, where vendors, mostly white folks, drove up and down the neighborhood streets in horse-drawn wagons, and later trucks, hawking meat, produce, and dairy goods. Other vendors, mostly African Americans, walked the same streets carrying baskets on their heads, shouting, "Nice, fresh vegetables!" "Irish potatoes!" "Fresh green beans!"

Peggy's father spent countless hours managing his hosiery manufacturing business. Like many men who worked indoors, he longed to experience the soul-stirring renewal of open land and fresh air, and his own personal escape from the factory was fishing. The funny thing was, he didn't like to clean fish, or eat them, so he always gave them away to somebody on his way home. At home, his job in the kitchen was to fry chicken every Sunday. After church, Peggy's mother got everything ready, the chicken cut up, and shallow bowls filled with milk and flour, then he stood at the stove and turned each piece as it bubbled in the hot grease, and set it over on a big platter when it was done just right.

People everywhere like to eat. But what's special in the South is that we also like to remember our meals, the people who serve them, and the people with whom we share them. "Mother filled our plates, and she didn't give us big servings, but wanted us to learn to eat everything," Peggy recalls. "I didn't like slaw very much, and one time I gradually scooted my slaw over until it kind of fell off the edge of

The beautifully crafted Lotz House was nearly destroyed when the Civil War Battle of Franklin, TN, raged around it. After the war, its owner restored it to its former glory as a residence and today it's a vital museum.

my plate. After a minute mother picked up the big bowl of slaw, reached over and dipped some more onto my plate, and gently said, 'Peggy, it looks like you need some more slaw.'"

Peggy and her brother had to clean their plate to get dessert. Their mother would always cut the pie, or whatever it was, and put their desert plate right there by the children's plates before they even started eating. Peggy says, "Of course, that made sure I cleaned my plate, because I sure wanted that dessert."

It seems that every town in the South has a food festival, and some places have a lot of them. Every event crowns a queen, closes the streets for a parade, provides music, and feeds whoever shows up hungry. Humboldt, TN, Chadbourn, NC, and Plant City, FL, all have strawberry festivals. Several places lay claim to the title of peach capitol of the world, including the whole state of Georgia, which also has an apple festival. Mississippi's long list of feasts range from crawfish in Biloxi to watermelon in Mize. Salley, SC, welcomes visitors to the annual Chitlin Strut. Several places in South Carolina are proud of their chicken bog. Everybody around there knows that a bog is a dish custom made for sitting on the porch and visiting with friends while the chicken simmers, then broth and rice are added, and that mixture cooks until the butter

A vegetable vendor drives through a well-to-do neighborhood in Virginia, selling his produce. (Courtesy of Library of Congress)

is added at the end. The bog is usually served with slaw and pickles, with sweet tea and home-churned ice cream for dessert, followed by more visiting and more time for the kids to play on the rope swing, until their weary heads nod off to sleep on the way home.

Among all those salutes to culinary excellence, there may be no single dish more reflective of Southern cuisine, with its quantity, creativity, and storied history, than burgoo. Basically, burgoo is a spicy stew. What are the ingredients? That varies. Where did it get its name? That's debatable. What we do know is that burgoo predates the Civil War, and while it may have been popular among both armies, it became a favorite in the Confederate camps. Once, in the midst of the long war, General John Hunt Morgan, of Tennessee, found himself with an undersupplied and hungry army, so he sent his troops out foraging. When the soldiers returned to camp, the cooks had a 500-pound iron kettle on the fire, and everything the troops brought back went into it. There was beef, chicken, sausage, and every imaginable vegetable. A French mercenary in their ranks added a mysterious blend of seasonings. He wouldn't tell the exact combination, but everybody said it was mainly salt and red pepper.

By the time the war was over, every army

cook had learned to make it, and veterans carried the tale home. In the years to come, burgoo was prepared in huge quantities for church dinners and town celebrations. Kentucky thoroughbred horse breeder E. R. Bradley owned a horse named Burgoo King, who won the Kentucky Derby. *The Progressive Farmer's Southern Cookbook* includes a recipe for burgoo made with 800 pounds of soup meat, four dozen squirrels, twenty-four gallons of corn, four bushels of onions, 240 pounds of chicken, fifteen bushels of potatoes, hundreds of pounds of other vegetables, and of course, a secret blend of spices, mainly salt and red pepper. To this day this timeless dish, which by its very nature draws throngs of people together, is featured at contests and gatherings called Burgoos.

When I was a young advertising whiz-bang on my first business trip to New Orleans, I had a few minutes to get something to eat in the airport. Just to try a little local cooking, I ordered a bowl of gumbo, expecting nothing special, maybe some sort of chicken soup with okra, similar to the gumbo I'd grown up eating out of a Campbell's can. After all, it was airport food. But, surprise! What I got was a whole blue crab looking up accusingly at me from a bowl of thick, spicy, seafood soup packed with vegetables. The only familiar thing in it was the okra. A smiling fellow named Bill at the next table saw me fumbling with the crab, as I slopped soup onto my new silk tie, and he kindly showed me how to eat the little monster so I could get to the soup. Then we talked about my family back home, and his family, whom he was meeting at the gate in a few minutes, and by the way, the gumbo was terrific. Thanks to Bill, I began to see that although people everywhere have their regional and local favorites, there's an attitude, a richness, a relationship with the food in the South that's uniquely embraceable.

And thanks to an anonymous chef back in the kitchen, I learned that good Southern Cookin', including world class gumbo, can be found anywhere, even in an airport.

Restaurants all over the country are known to sprinkle their menus with Southern this and Southern that. Sure, the Gulf shrimp on a Chicago menu came from the Gulf. And the "Real Carolina Barbecue" at a Minnesota eatery has a vinegar-based sauce similar to the ones served in Columbia and Charleston. On the other hand, putting garlic and black pepper on a steak in Akron doesn't make it a Louisiana sirloin. Some dishes and some names on menus are nothing more than attempts to borrow a little Southern charm. But it's not food alone that makes a genuine Southern restaurant genuinely Southern. In fact, when it comes to delivering a genuinely Dixie experience, the hospitality of a place is just as important as the menu, the ingredients, and the cooking methods.

Consider Waffle House. We might think it couldn't have any kind of quaint Southern charm, because it's a chain, and chain restaurants can be so cold. But before Waffle House was a chain, it was a neighborhood restaurant started by two friends in a suburb of Atlanta. Their idea was to cook food to order, in a kitchen out front, in full view, to serve it quickly on real dishes, and to make everybody feel welcome.

And how's that working, now that they have 1500 restaurants? Before customers get both feet in the door they'll be greeted with a loud, "Good morning," from at least two of the servers, who all smile while they work. Diners chat from one table to another. They exchange newspapers and gardening tips. The waitress is quick to tell you her son is on the grill today and he makes the fluffiest omelets in the world. She's even likely to remember that you prefer wheat toast and like your bacon extra crispy.

At restaurants like that, when one of the regular customers has a birthday, one of the crew is likely to bake him a cake at home and bring it in. They might give him a bag full of birthday cards and a funny coffee cup, and sing "Happy Birthday" so loudly, out-of-tune, and silly that everybody in the place laughs until they cry. It's not always like that. There's not always a birthday. But otherwise, yes, it's always like that. Like home. Where people are happy to see each other.

In fact, there may be nothing particularly Southern about the food in Southern cafés. A good case could be made for a patty melt being a Northern invention. Hash brown potatoes, the signature dish at Waffle House, were named by a guy who owned a Boston cooking school and wrote cookbooks. Yes, you can order grits and pork chops at some Southern eateries twenty-four hours a day, but it's not a question of whether the dishes are Southern. It's the feel of the place. It's people loving each other and sharing a little bit of life. When the servers pick up a tip, they say, "Thank you," like it's the best thing that ever happened to them. And when their customers leave, they holler, "Bye bye, ya'll," and, "Come back." That's pretty much the way it's always been around the tables in Dixie's homes, only without the tips.

But wait, aren't today's Southern families as busy as anyone else? Aren't they awash with changing technology, education, yoga, tailgating, and the kids' ballet lessons and soccer practices? Sure. In fact, with new leather sofas now sharing the fireside with time-worn antiques, there's a reborn glory in Southern homes. Some families sit down to eat on scarred and repainted heirloom tables from who-knows-how-long ago, and some dine on shiny tables fresh from the furniture store. Some people quietly fill their plates every evening under the gaze of ancestors in gilded frames, while some live such busy lives that Mama has to demand that we set our schedules and electronic devices aside to sit down to a meal together.

Then there are the cousins, some are distant, and some closer than siblings. But it's like no time has passed, when we all show up with a special dish and say how good it is, then we swap the recipes, and then we swap stories about the aunts and uncles and the ones who aren't here this year. Then we laugh and watch the little ones, and there, for a while, everything is all right. Just being with them is a balm for the heart.

So, although mealtime is pretty much the same everywhere, all the time, when we gather for a meal in the South, it's a real meal. It's an old, favorite song, conjuring up memories of other fine meals we've shared with loved ones, amid smiles, laughter, and the simple warmth of being in a familiar embrace. Last summer's stories blend with those from the last century like an unfolding family quilt. There's an ancient voice always whispering, never letting us forget that we're part of a long and beautiful story.

Sometimes, everything in that story moves in slow motion. That's why a busy father can be seen in a Hawaiian shirt on Christmas Eve, roasting pans full of ducks in the oven, while he's smoking a pork butt and grilling vegetables on the patio, playing a game of pool with his son-in-law, and pouring wine for a room full of loves ones, and it all seems effortless. Whether Southerners are growing tomatoes, frying a mess of catfish, or baking a pie, it takes as long as it takes. You can't hurry love.

You see, food is made special by the people who enjoy it, and Southern Cookin' can't be separated from Southern hospitality. It's about hosting and welcoming and creating something wonderful for the people we love, served with a hearty helping of "bless your heart." Nobody, and I mean nobody, ever comes to the house without being offered something to eat and drink. We might be down to one slice of bread, but that slice of bread is yours.

One evening when I was in my early twenties, I'd been down to the pond on our little rented farm to hunt frogs, and had six real nice pairs of legs. When I put them on to boil, I decided I didn't want to eat them alone. So I put the lid on the cold pot of frog legs, jumped into the car, and drove over to the home of my friends John and Jan, who'd been married just a short time. They answered the door, and I held up the pan and asked with a big smile, "Hey, you all want to help me eat some frog legs?" They looked at each other, then back at me, and then laughed so hard I thought they'd never stop. Finally, John caught his breath and said, "Come in here." I followed them into the kitchen, and there on a plate was package of saltine crackers and one slice of baloney cut into four sections.

"We were just sitting down to eat," Jan said. "This is all we have."

"And I don't get paid until tomorrow," John added.

We all laughed some more, put the frog legs on the stove to boil, and then sat down to one of the oddest and most memorable meals we've ever had.

Today, most people wouldn't dream of "stopping by" to visit without calling first, because we're all so busy. But there was a time, before cell phones and ear buds, when folks from near and far used to show up unannounced for a visit. Hard to imagine, isn't it? And no matter what Aunt Floy and Uncle Roy were doing, they'd drop it to get their visitors a cup of coffee and a piece of pie. Company, expected or not, was always welcome to come in and set a spell. That's how people got the news from home. That's how the children learned to love their families, and more important, that how one generation

after another learned how to treat folks who stop by.

It's like the time when I was a little boy and our family stopped by Uncle Al's house. After greeting us he looked into his fridge, saw that he had only one beer, and asked my dad if he'd like to split it. Of course, dad didn't want to split a beer; he wanted a whole one. But he just nodded and said that would be real nice, and while our two families sat there visiting at the yellow Formica kitchen table, drinking lemonade, dad and Uncle Al shared two little juice glasses of beer. While we may not "stop by" like we once did, remembered scenes like that, and the love they embody, still linger in the Southern psyche.

The funny thing about hospitality, it works both ways. If I baked cookies last night, I'd bring you some. If you're passing through our town, we expect you to stop and see us. And we'll send you on your way with a sandwich or a jar of strawberry jam. In fact, the jam will probably be in the same jar in which you gave us some pepper jelly when we passed through your town last year.

Right now, in some Southern home, tucked away in a walnut bookcase, is a book with a torn spine, and inside that book is a recipe written in pencil on the back of an envelope with a faded three-cent stamp. It's stained with years of butter and milk, and infused with the joy of cooking something wonderful for people who love each other. There between the lines are all the family cooks, butchers, bakers, and gardeners who went before. There, on that yellowed page are all the dreams for little ones to grow up well-fed and healthy. There, among the measures and misspelled instructions are the ties that bind hearts in love across the generations. In the end, the story of Southern food is the story of the people who share it. And that's what makes Southern Cookin' so good.

Bibliography

Butler, Cleora. *Cleora's Kitchens: Eight Decades of Great American Foods.* Tulsa: Council Oaks Books, Ltd., 1985.

Diamond, Jared. *Guns, Germs, and Steel: The Fates of Human Societies.* New York: W. W. Norton & Co. 1999.

Gates, Henry Louis, Jr., ed. *Classic Slave Narratives.* New York: New American Library, 2002.

Hakala, Sue. *Drought Gardening.* Charlotte: Garden Way Associates, 1981.

Helton, Ginger and Susan Van Riper, ed. *Hermitage Hospitality.* Nashville: Aurora Publishers, 1970.

Hill, Sallie F. *The Progressive Farmer's Southern Cookbook.* Birmingham: Birmingham Printing Company Division of the Progressive Farmer Company, 1961.

Hobson, Phyllis. *Easy Game Cookery.* Charlotte: Garden Way Associates, 1980.

Hobson, Phyllis. *Butchering Livestock at Home.* Charlotte: Garden Way Associates, 1981.

Howell, Leon and Ridgeway, Donna, ed. *United State Bi-Centennial Commemorative Cookbook 1776-1976.* Kansas City: Commemorative Cookbooks, 1972.

Johnston, Joe. *Necessary Evil: Missouri's Last Vigilante.* St. Louis: Missouri History Museum, 2014.

Maury, Anne Fontaine. *Intimate Virginia: A Century of Maury Travels by Land and Sea.* Richmond: The Dietz Press, 1941.

McCullouch, Edward P., *The Native Americans in Williamson County, Tennessee: Through the Date of the Last Permanent Village Settlement, Circa 1450.* Nashville: Unlimited Publishing, LLC, 2011.

Neely, Jeremy. *The Border Between Them: Violence and Reconciliation on the Kansas-Missouri Line.* Columbia: University of Missouri Press, 2007.

Nevin, David. *The Old West: The Texans.* New York: Time-Life Books, 1982.

Nichols, Nell B., ed. *Freezing & Canning Cookbook: Prized Recipes from the Farms of America.* Garden City: Doubleday & Co., 1973.

Reiter, Joan Swallow. *The Old West: The Women.* New York: Time-Life Books, 1982.

Rutledge, Sarah. *The Carolina Housewife.* Charleston: W. R. Babcock, 1847.

Tyree, Marion Cabell, ed. *Housekeeping in Old Virginia.* Louisville: John P. Morton and Company, 1879.

Wayne, Michael. *The Reshaping of Plantation Society, The Natchez District 1860-80.* Urbana: University of Illinois Press, 1990.

The War of the Rebellion: A Compilation of the Official Records of the Union and Confederate Armies. Washington: Government Printing Office, 1880.

Index